VW Golf

Other Titles in the Crowood AutoClassic Series

VW Golf

With Scirocco, Corrado and Karmann convertible derivatives

James Ruppert

Foreword by **Giorgetto Giugiaro**

First published in 1996 by
The Crowood Press Ltd
Ramsbury, Marlborough
Wiltshire SN8 2HR

British Library Cataloguing-in-Publication Data
A catalogue record for this book is available from the British
Library

ISBN 1 85223 996 4

Picture Credits
ITALDESIGN, Volkswagen GB & AG, James Ruppert, GTi Engineering,
Karmann AG, Kamei, Zender, R & A Designs.

Printed and bound by BPC Books Ltd, Aylesbury

Contents

Foreword

Whenever I see an original model Golf on the road I feel elated. I was full of enthusiasm when I designed the Golf more than twenty years ago because Volkswagen gave me complete freedom – combined with a tight schedule, this produced a simple yet original design.

The Golf's unique two-box shape was stylish and practical, but it looked nothing like a station wagon. Of course, some design details had to change during development, especially as the Golf had to comply with American regulations, so the windscreen became more upright and the bonnet was lengthened. Cost constraints also meant that the original rectangular headlights were replaced with round ones.

If I had the opportunity to modify the Golf, I would change very little. Some of the lines could be softened, but otherwise I think that the dimensions and proportions are perfect. As the heir to the Beetle, the Golf fully reflects my philosophy of simple forms and clean lines, which is the basis for all my creations.

Giorgetto Giugiaro,
Designer of the Original and Best Golf

Acknowledgements

I am most grateful to Giorgetto Giugiaro for taking the time to pen a few words about one of his greatest creations. That would not have been possible, and neither would the exclusive Italdesign archive photographs have been located if Silvia Collazuol had not been so very helpful. Alexander Paul at Karmann very kindly arranged exclusive access to their excellent museum at short notice.

All the specialist UK Volkswagen tuners were very helpful: Tim Stiles, Autocavan, Brian Ricketts and GTi Engineering all very kindly provided lots of important information and pictures. Thanks also to Brian Smith of Scotford for Kamei pictures, Eurostyling for the Zender information, and Richard Walker at R&A Designs.

Hats off to the very well run Club GTI – and to Mick Clements in particular, who put me in contact with members prepared to put up with me mucking about for hours on end with my box brownie: Colin Stone, Mike Smith, John McGrath and John Wintle. Foyes Motor Company kindly let me photograph a Rallye.

I apologize to those who responded to my appeal for help but whose cars, for reasons of space, have not been included. I should also like to thank Simon Alhadi, John Williams and Neil Beaney who provided useful information. Nick Carter at Max Communications came up with contemporary racing photographs very quickly. Paul Buckett at Volkswagen GB was helpful too. Thanks to John Tipler, fellow Crowood author and supremely talented motor journalist, who suggested I write the book, and to Peter Burton at Crowood for being so patient.

Mrs Ruppert made sure we caught the ferry, never got lost on the way to Wolfsburg, made lots of important suggestions and put up with all sorts of Golf related nonsense for six months. I am also very grateful to my parents who have bought Volkswagens since the early 1980s and let me drive and dent them.

Introduction

The original Volkswagen Golf was perfect. Ask Giorgetto Giugiaro – or read his foreword. Few cars have hit the spot the way that the Golf did in 1974. Like all the best automotive designs – and in particular the Mini 15 years before – it emerged as a fully formed motor car. In terms of packaging, build quality and sheer purity of purpose the Golf set extremely high standards. It remains one of the very few cars that have made a huge difference to the way vehicles are styled and packaged, and how they perform. Remarkably, it also spawned a whole range of related but distinct models, like the Scirocco, Jetta, Corrado and Golf convertible.

The Golf sent shock waves through the industry as manufacturers with inadequate and impractical saloons had to think again, which meant thinking hatchback. Likewise the GTI redefined the affordable sports car – practical, faster and more fun than anything that had gone before – and in the process created the 'hot hatch'. Meanwhile Karmann's cabriolet killed off all those creaky old 1960s roadsters and proved that open air cars could be comfortable, leakproof and reliable. The Jetta established that a boot can never be too big, while the stylish Scirocco demonstrated beyond reasonable doubt that the coupé concept was still alive and flourishing. And finally there was the ultimate variation on the Golf theme: the Corrado. In VR6 form it was the fastest Volkswagen of all. It may have been prematurely snuffed out, but at least it burned brightly for a while.

The Golf has always been a car that people want to buy. It was probably the first true world car – it was built on several continents and made sense in so many diverse markets. Clearly the Golf came as a huge relief to Volkswagen, who had been shackled to the Beetle for so long.

This book is not a tuner's handbook, nor a sycophantic and dry official history. It is an opinionated and occasionally irreverent assessment of the model and its close relations, livened up with some eye popping pictures. Any oversights or mistakes are entirely my fault. All the opinions, conclusions and ravings are mine too. I also take full responsibility for the attack on the cult of the Beetle.

By the time you read this book, the shape of the new Golf will be known and maybe launched, driven and discontinued, but I do not think it will matter or make this book obsolete. Underneath it all, the engine, suspension and overall concept can be traced to the original 1974 model. That is why this book is a celebration of the Golf's formative years, its consolidation with the Mark 2 and subsequent decline with the Mark 3.

Why interfere with a successful formula? Well, that formula does not work any more – all the other manufacturers have produced their own antidotes. What is really worrying, however, is that the imminent Mark 4 will be just another re-skin. Come on, Volkswagen. Things are never going to be as bad as the last days of the Beetle, so it will not hurt to take another Beetle-sized gamble to replace the fading Golf. All it will take is a blank design screen, some lateral thinking and the talented Signor Giugiaro.

1   Blame it on the Beetle

'It is too ugly and too noisy' – Sir William Rootes.

In 1961 Volkswagen thought they had produced a new range of models that would take over from the hugely successful Beetle. Instead, the Type 3 was a flop and for the next decade the company floundered from one misconceived model to another. In order to understand where Volkswagen went so right with the Golf, it is crucial to chart their numerous

Beetle and Golf together – nothing in common apart from a Volkswagen badge – seen here with Dr Ferry Porsche. His father designed the Beetle and Ferry Porsche repeatedly tried to help Volkswagen to replace it.

misadventures in between times. So how did Volkswagen get into this mess? The answer is simple – the Beetle.

IN THE BEGINNING, THE BEETLE

Marching into Poland and world domination were not yet on the agenda when Hitler proposed a 'people's car'. Dr Porsche's Type 60 – a hotchpotch of 1930s technology and fashionable streamline design, which could be traced to contemporary Tatras and the rear engined Mercedes – perfectly fitted the requirements. The vehicle was named the KdF Wagen from the initials of the German Labour Front. In 1938 a production plant – the Volks-

wagenwerke or 'people's car factory' – was built on a soggy plain in Wolfsburg. The new car was to be financed by a savings plan to which 270,000 had subscribed by 1939. Despite collecting the red stamps featuring the white image of the KdF and faithfully sticking them into savings books, none of the 'people' actually got to own one.

The Second World War may have hindered civilian car production, but it inspired Porsche to design numerous military versions. Best known were the Schwimmwagen, which was an amphibious four wheel drive vehicle, and the Kübelwagen, essentially a Jeep. The latter served with distinction in all the theatres of war under extreme conditions, was praised by Rommel in the desert campaigns and proved adept at traversing

This is the cover of the brochure that enticed Germans to join an unusual savings scheme. Collect enough stamps and a brand new KdF-Wagen was the reward. However, no one ever received a Beetle, partly because there was a war on, but mostly because Volkswagen never got around to building any civilian vehicles.

snow on the Eastern Front.

Over 80,000 military chassis were built, proving just how versatile and sound the original design was. These qualities inevitably contributed to the Beetle's longevity and adaptability, as the basic theme was stretched to breaking point over the next thirty years. In 1945, however, Volkswagen did not have much of a future to look forward to. A ruined factory and the fact that no KdF Wagen had ever been built did not bode well. Luckily, a combination of the British and the Beetle saved the day.

What the army found when they arrived was a half built city called KdF-Stadt, which they promptly renamed Wolfsburg after the nearby castle. They did not like the name Volkswagen, so they called the factory the Wolfsburg Motor Works. The Royal Electrical and Mechanical Engineers were dispatched to see whether vehicle production could be recommenced. They uncovered a single surviving prototype KdF Wagen, which proved useful as a demonstration vehicle for the military authorities. Major Ivan Hirst was put in charge and he managed to galvanize the small workforce into action. Initially repairing vehicles, they managed to assemble some Kübelwagens from surviving parts, but since the body presses for the KdF still existed, serious production began for the first time in late 1945. By the end of that year they had begun to satisfy the urgent need for light transport, turning out 1,785 vehicles for the British Army and the German post office.

Hirst had achieved the impossible and as output topped 10,000 in 1946 he skilfully foiled attempts to dismantle the factory in lieu of war reparations and ship it to Australia. The company's survival may also be attributed to the misjudgement of another Englishman, Sir William Rootes. When visiting the ruins of the Wolfsburg

Major Ivan Hirst, a forgotten hero. Volkswagen rightly give him full credit for saving the company and kick starting the German economy.

factory as the head of the Rootes Commission he was unimpressed and recommended demolition 'or it will collapse of its own inertia within two years'. The Commission also stated that 'the vehicle does not meet the fundamental technical requirements of a motor car. As regards performance and design it is quite unattractive to the average motor car buyer. It is too ugly and too noisy.' They concluded: 'to build the car commercially would be a completely uneconomic enterprise'.

Hindsight is a wonderful thing and in the ruined surroundings of a defeated country the Beetle (as it was not yet called) could not have looked an attractive proposition. However, Rootes and all the other British manufacturers were ignoring the President of the Board of Trade, Sir Stafford Cripps, who had some interesting proposals for the industry in the prevailing post war climate. Speaking at a Society of Motor Manufacturers' and Traders' dinner in November 1945 he said: 'We must provide a cheap, tough, good-looking car of decent size – not the sort of car we have hitherto produced for smooth roads and short journeys in this country – and we must produce them in sufficient quantities to get the benefits of mass production.' He

could almost have been planning the Golf thirty years hence, but his remarks adequately described the fledgling Beetle. And when he added 'we cannot succeed in getting the volume of exports we must have if we disperse our efforts over numberless types and makes' this was a clear reference to the benefits of following a one-model policy. British industry did not embrace that principle, but Major Ivan Hirst did.

Hirst not only supervised production as it climbed rapidly, but also made some vital decisions. One was the retention of the pre war 'V over W' emblem and with it the adoption of the Volkswagen name, as 'Wolfsburg Motor Works' had never really

Against all the odds Major Hirst drives the 1000th Beetle off the production line. This ceremony would become commonplace over the coming years as production records were regularly broken and Volkswagen chalked up a million Beetle sales.

Managing director Heinrich Nordhoff, who was responsible for the huge and rapid growth of Volkswagen, announcing another Beetle landmark. Ten years later he would be accused of building just 'one dying model'.

caught on. Second was the appointment in 1948 of the former Opel executive Heinrich Nordhoff as the first civilian boss. In 1949, two significant events occurred as the first Beetle was shipped to America and control was handed over to the Germans. A year later the 100,000th Beetle had been built – Volkswagen were on their way.

POST WAR MIRACLE

Nordhoff proved to be the perfect dictatorial boss for these difficult times. He had the foresight to establish Volkswagen of America and capitalize on the car's success in that huge export market. Volkswagen also went global, establishing assembly plants in Brazil, Australia, Belgium, Ireland, Mexico, New Zealand, the Philippines and South Africa. Just as crucial was an agreement signed with Porsche whereby Volkswagen retained their design services, but they were prevented from building a rival of their own – although Porsche seemed happy enough developing the Beetle into a series of legendary sports cars.

Nordhoff largely continued where Hirst left off, sticking stubbornly to a one model policy and to his favourite motto, 'change only to improve'. Variations on the Beetle theme amounted to the light commercial Type 2 or Kombi from 1951 and the pretty Karmann-Ghia coupé from 1955 and cabriolet from 1967. Underneath though they were still Beetles. And when a Beetle did change, blink and you could miss the subtle update – like the pull heating control replaced by a rotary knob (1953) or the leatherette headlining (1963). Of course, there were some more significant changes, and by the time the last Beetle left the Wolfsburg production line 78,000 separate modifications had been made. Yet fundamental shortcomings like restricted interior space, lacklustre performance and dicey handling were never properly addressed.

By 1960 the Beetle dream was starting to look decidedly shaky. Just as Volkswagen became a public company – with the West German government and the state of Lower Saxony each holding 20 per cent of shares and employees getting one free and an option on nine others – there was a strike in Hanover. It lasted for 24 hours and was Volkswagen's first taste of industrial action. Critics started to whisper that Nordhoff was building a dying model. Then in 1961 all those disappointed KdF stamp buyers who had banded together and filed a lawsuit against the company finally reached a settlement. Volkswagen offered them either DM100 in cash or DM600 off the price of a new Beetle. Into this less than welcoming atmosphere came the Type 3.

After the jelly mould Beetle, the Type 3 was a traditional three box that was later joined by a fast-back and the estate. Underneath lurked a rear engined Bug. The first of many unsuccessful attempts by Volkswagen to replace their most successful saloon.

TYPECAST

There was no disguising the Beetle origins of the Type 3 launched in 1961. It was the third incarnation of the basic Beetle concept. On the surface it looked contemporary with almost conventional three box styling for the saloon and a two box layout for the estate. Inside it was decidedly roomy and there was usable luggage space too. Other innovations included an automatic choke and all synchromesh gearbox. Nevertheless, a 6-volt electrical system and drum brakes were hardly the cutting edge. The engine may well have been 1,500cc, but it was still air cooled and mounted at the back of the car.

The best that can be said for the Type 3 is that it was faster than a Beetle, especially the hot rod 'S' version from 1965 with an extra carburettor and 85mph (137kph) on tap. There were radical updates in 1966 with the installation of a new 1,600cc fastback model with a swooping roof. In spite of yet more improvements throughout the late 1960s that included fuel injection, dual circuit brakes and MacPherson front suspension, sales struggled to 1.8 million – a relative failure in Volkswagen terms. Sadly the anonymous Type 3 was not the answer – everyone knew it and just kept on buying Beetles.

Volkswagen's last attempt in 1968 to transform the Beetle into a modern motor car also ended in failure. The Type 4 designation gave the game away, as the 411 and later 412 amounted to little more than a great big Type 3, with a bigger engine. By lengthening the wheelbase there was finally room for four doors. Coils on the rear suspension meant that handling was much tidier and overall it was not a bad attempt at a bang up to date Beetle. But Volkswagen should have known better. By

Here the Beetle concept is stretched to breaking point in the shape of the 411, later refined into the facelifted 412. Lots more room, but still air cooled and unforgivably ugly. Another dud.

sticking to outmoded, air cooled, rear wheel drive, rear engine technology the company proved that it was in the automotive dark ages. Front wheel drive was the way to go and the 411 could not begin to compete with the likes of the Renault 16, or even the well packaged but flawed Austin Maxi. Surprisingly, Pininfarina were partly guilty for producing a saloon that looked like a war time tin top Kübelwagen. Even the Variant estate version was only vaguely practical as it was restricted to just two doors.

The styling was almost as non existent as the customers; Volkswagen found it hard to convince anyone that a 411 was worth buying. As this disastrous model was launched the man responsible for the Volkswagen success story, Heinrich Nordhoff, died. It was the end of an era and if the company was going to survive there had to be fresh ideas, new models and wholesale changes.

Volkswagen had started to assemble the ill fitting pieces of the recovery jigsaw during the 1960s. In 1965 they started to build what would become the motor industry's largest wind tunnel, not that the Beetle benefited much from aerodynamics. Its distinctive shape never improved on a 0.44 drag coefficient, so models of the future could only get better. Most important of all, Volkswagen acquired from Daimler the capital stock of the legendary Auto-Union GMbH in Ingolstadt. With that came the Audi range and some interesting models and projects that would allow Volkswagen to take a giant leap forward. But first they stumbled two steps back with the K70.

OASIS OR MIRAGE?

A project being developed by NSU at the time of the take-over was a four door saloon. Based on the chassis of the ill fated rotary engined Ro80 model, the K70 featured more conventional technology, but when badged as a Volkswagen in 1970, it was revolutionary – their first water cooled engined car, their first front engined car and their first front wheel drive car.

Sadly, sales came a very poor second. Over five years they sold a paltry 211,100. No part was ever used on another Volkswagen and it stands very alone as an interesting pointer to the future, even if it did confuse traditional Volkswagen buyers. At least it proved that Volkswagen were capable of breaking the Beetle mould even if they had to use the ideas of a recently acquired manufacturer. This approach paid off when Volkswagen decided to look at what their other subsidiary, Audi, were up to.

HOLE IN ONE

The upmarket, medium sized 80 with Audi's own overhead camshaft engines turned out to be the perfect basis for an all new Volkswagen. Genius Italian designer Giugiaro was commissioned to style the car and the result was the Passat in 1973. A dull but always worthy stalwart of the Volkswagen range, it proved to be as reliable as the Beetle but beat it in terms of practicality and performance, offering a wide range of hatchback, saloon and estate variants. All it really lacked, which the Beetle had in plenty, was personality. Volkswagen's master stroke was to scale down the Passat concept into the Golf. The rest is history.

The Volkswagen Golf certainly has a top five placing when looking at the most influential models in the history of motoring. Frequently copied, never bettered and still evolving, the Golf put Volkswagen back on

Volkswagen's first water-cooled car, a re-badged NSU K70. As the Volkswagen K70 it failed to live up to expectations, but allowed the company to dip its toes into water and face a front engined future.

Volkswagen finally build a car that looks as though it was designed in the late twentieth century. Body by Giugiaro, engine donated by the Audi 80, front wheel drive chassis and hatchback body – the Passat was the blueprint for the most successful range of cars ever.

a firm financial footing and gave them a future. So 1975 has to be regarded as the year when the Volkswagen story starts all over again, although just three years before the future had looked very bleak. Indeed, Volkswagen were still trying to fob us off with the 'Marathon' special edition Beetle to celebrate the fact that it had overtaken the Ford Model T when the sales figures tipped 15,007,034. But by the time the Beetle had sold that many it was well and truly obsolete. The Golf did not come a moment too soon, yet it did not kill off the Beetle. Indeed, the Beetle lived on until 1978 in Germany and continues a long period of retirement in Mexico where the Puebla plant built the 21 millionth Beetle in 1992 and is cantering towards 22 million

at the time of writing. The Beetle is not yet dead and – most worrying of all – looks set for a dramatic reincarnation as the Concept 1.

THE BEETLES ARE BACK

In the prevailing retrospective styling climate of 1994 Volkswagen took the decision to develop and ultimately produce the Concept 1. In the process they cancelled a sensible super-mini called the Chico and wrote off £160m worth of investment. The Concept is Golf sized but is nowhere near as well packaged. Rear seat passengers will get neck ache, there is precious little room for luggage and the proposed diesel

Back to Beetle basics with the Concept 1. The Retro way forward, or a couple of steps back?

Coming soon, the revised Concept. A bigger, better Beetle, but who really needs it?

and electric hybrid power plants might just fit under the bonnet, but performance is always going to be a last priority. The Concept is an easy target for ridicule and is due in 1999 when retrospective frivolity will be out of fashion.

Despite this, in October 1995 at the Tokyo Motor Show the company unveiled an updated design study of the Concept that was 9.5in (240mm) longer and 2.8in (70mm) wider. Bigger and better with a transversely mounted petrol engine, rather than some hybrid power plant, the car was being put into production and is likely to be with us even sooner – conclusive proof that Volkswagen have lost the plot and do not need to rehash an old favourite when they run short of ideas. Last time they were in such a mess, Volkswagen produced a bold, innovative and exciting new concept called the Golf. So the Beetle may yet come back to haunt Volkswagen, and worst of all it might even stifle any future development of the Golf.

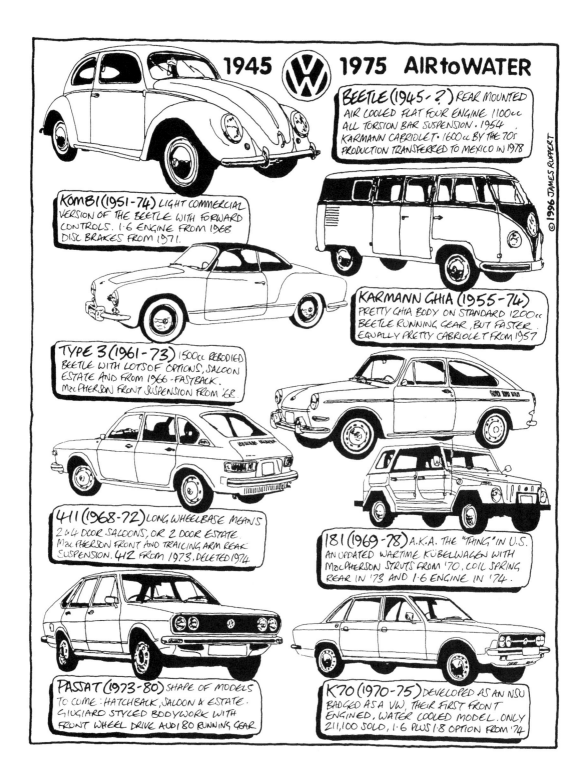

1945 1975 AIR to WATER

© 1996 JAMES RUPPERT

BEETLE (1945-?) REAR MOUNTED AIR COOLED FLAT FOUR ENGINE 1100cc ALL TORSION BAR SUSPENSION. 1954 KARMANN CABRIOLET. 1600cc BY THE 70's PRODUCTION TRANSFERRED TO MEXICO IN 1978

KOMBI (1951-74) LIGHT COMMERCIAL VERSION OF THE BEETLE WITH FORWARD CONTROLS. 1.6 ENGINE FROM 1968 DISC BRAKES FROM 1971.

KARMANN GHIA (1955-74) PRETTY GHIA BODY ON STANDARD 1200cc BEETLE RUNNING GEAR, BUT FASTER. EQUALLY PRETTY CABRIOLET FROM 1957

TYPE 3 (1961-73) 1500cc REBODIED BEETLE WITH LOTS OF OPTIONS, SALOON ESTATE AND FROM 1966-FASTBACK. MacPHERSON FRONT SUSPENSION FROM '68.

411 (1968-72) LONG WHEELBASE MEANS 2&4 DOOR SALOONS, OR 2 DOOR ESTATE. MacPHERSON FRONT AND TRAILING ARM REAR SUSPENSION. 412 FROM 1973, DELETED 1974.

181 (1969-78) A.K.A. THE "THING" IN U.S. AN UPDATED WARTIME KÜBELWAGEN WITH MacPHERSON STRUTS FROM '70, COIL SPRING REAR IN '73 AND 1.6 ENGINE IN '74.

PASSAT (1973-80) SHAPE OF MODELS TO COME: HATCHBACK, SALOON & ESTATE. GIUGIARO STYLED BODYWORK WITH FRONT WHEEL DRIVE AUDI 80 RUNNING GEAR

K70 (1970-75) DEVELOPED AS AN NSU BADGED AS A VW, THEIR FIRST FRONT ENGINED, WATER COOLED MODEL. ONLY 211,100 SOLD. 1.6 PLUS 1.8 OPTION FROM '74

2 The Golf Hatched

'The origami school of car design' – Uwe Bahnsen, Ford design chief.

In 1969, Volkswagen President Kurt Lotz was taking notes at the Turin Motor Show. He was talking to journalists and asking what everyone thought of the prototypes and design studies on the coachbuilders' stands, and he jotted down the names of all the most striking and original stylists. After a while he glanced down at his short-list to discover that four of the six models

What the Golf could have looked like. The 1969 EA266 was a radical two box shape. It was a hatchback too, the tailgate being usefully deep, the accommodation generous and the styling quite pleasing. Unfortunately, lurking under the boot floor was an air cooled Beetle engine driving the rear wheels, so back to the drawing board.

were designed by Giorgetto Giugiaro.

GIUGIARO'S GENIUS

Giugiaro was born on 7 August 1938 and quickly acquired the artistic skills of his family. His grandfather, Luigi, frescoed villas and churches in the Cuneo region and the young Giugiaro would often help out. Transferring the designs from cardboard templates onto the wall by perforating the board and rubbing coal dust through the holes taught him the rigid disciplines involved in executing a design – it was only when the outline had been painstakingly established that the colourful and detailed fresco work could begin. His mother, Maria, was an accomplished seamstress and Giugiaro was constantly intrigued by her transformation of a simple one-dimensional drawing into a beautiful dress. Indeed, Giugiaro has even compared the art of dressmaking with car design as cutting and sewing a piece of fabric is 'not all that unlike cutting and welding a piece of sheet metal to give life to a bodywork'.

At fourteen, Giugiaro had his secondary school diploma and moved to Turin to study art and technical drawing. At the art academy's end of year show in 1955 his automotive work came to the attention of Fiat designer Dante Giacosa and led directly to his being employed by the Special Cars Styling Department. After a useful if quiet spell within that huge conglomerate, he moved to specialist coachbuilders Bertone in 1959, where he established his reputation as a ground breaking designer. By 1960 two of his designs had been produced to worldwide acclaim in the shape of the Ferrari 250 GT and the Alfa Giulia GT, the latter entering production almost immediately. In 1965 he moved to Ghia as head of their Styling and Design Centre. Despite

two sports car masterpieces, the Maserati Ghibli and De Tomaso Mangusta, relations with the new owner, De Tomaso, soured and this hastened the designer's departure. On 7 February 1967 Giugiaro struck out on his own and founded Ital Styling.

SUD CONNECTION

Giugiaro's consultancy services were in demand, leading directly to the creation of Italdesign and the most important commission to date from Alfa Romeo. This was no one off styling exercise or limited production supercar, but the legendary Alfasud – a mass market car to be made in a new factory in the south of Italy. In charge of the project was Rudolf Hruska, while Giugiaro and Italdesign had to refine the design, all the engineering, build the prototypes and see the project right through to the tooling stage.

Hruska's design brief was exacting, requiring a compact car that was aerodynamic, roomy and structurally strong. It also had to be a sound basis for a number of spin off models including a coupé, estate and spider. In order to maximize interior space Giugiaro had opted for a two box shape with a high, cut off tail. Overall he had produced a very clean and uncluttered design. As a package, the Alfasud was a brilliant success; for many buyers the appeal was largely practical as roominess and load capacity were unsurpassed by any contemporary model. Not only that, the front wheel drive layout and its fine chassis meant superb handling for the enthusiastic motorist. The Alfasud was a true design classic that stayed in production until 1983. The only problems were its disastrous build quality and the fact that it was not initially a hatchback.

PASSAT PREVIEW

The Alfasud has to be seen as the father of the Golf. Take a look at an Italdesign body mock up from around 1968 with round headlights and there are no doubts that the Sud must have been a big influence on the Golf. This is hardly surprising when Giugiaro relates the words used by Kurt Lotz when he turned up at the Italdesign

stand in 1969 and said 'Do what you want, but do it fast.' The commission was to design a mid range model that would eventually turn into the Passat. Giugiaro was indeed fast and delivered a detailed presentation by May 1970.

The radical design – which resembled a larger scale Golf – frightened Volkswagen management and new president Rudolf Leidling in particular. That car was

Back at the drawing board, Volkswagen came up with the EA276 in 1969. The hatchback format was now set, with short overhangs and a long roof with a stubby tail. At last, the package featured a front engine, with front wheel drive and water cooled. A proper pre-Golf awaiting the magic touch of Giugiaro.

The Golf Hatched

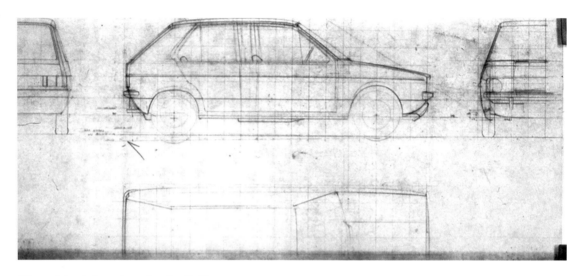

The original elevations for the Golf.

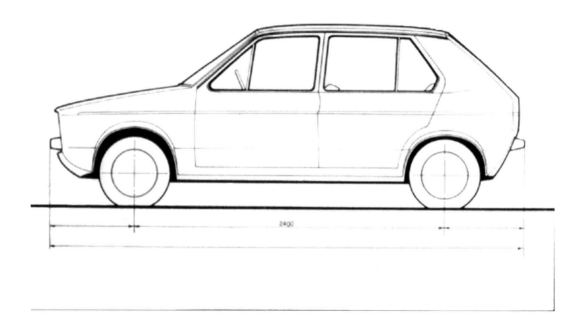

Worked up into a scaled dimensional drawing.

24

From which a full size buck is made.

The distinctive rear pillar and revolutionary wrap-around tailgate are created. Not that a third window was considered on a 5-door buck.

The buck is refined by the stylists.

cancelled and Giugiaro was asked to base the Passat on the existing Audi 80. As a result it looked a bit of a mess with 80 front end, doors and chassis plus the rear end of the original proposal grafted on. Giugiaro has never been happy with the compromise and it explains why, despite solid sales, the Passat has always lacked real flair. To this day, Volkswagen's attempt at a bigger, up market model has always fallen short of buyers' expectations, so the fundamental concept must be wrong. However, some good did come of that fateful meeting.

GOLF SHAPES UP

Volkswagen asked Giugiaro to plan the model that would become the Golf and once again time was of the essence. Wolfsburg did not require any preliminary sketches, or drawings for approval, all they wanted was a full size model as soon as possible. Within just three months Italdesign had delivered a model of the proposed Golf and Wolfsburg gave the project a go-ahead within days. Volkswagen were fully committed to the project and even made a

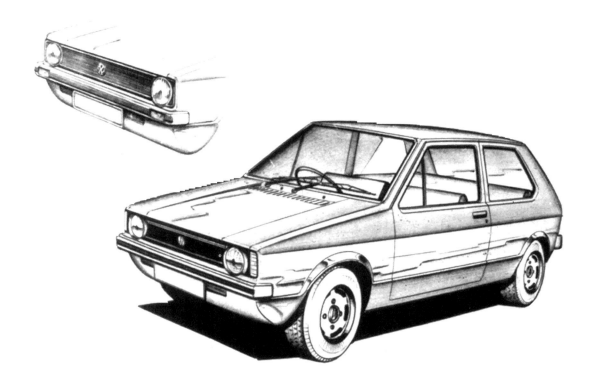

Alternative front end treatments. The indicators were finally sited on the bumper.

company aeroplane available so that Giugiaro could commute between Turin and Wolfsburg. His complete control of the project meant that the purity of the original shape survived almost intact. But once Volkswagen had decided to export the Golf to America prevailing regulations had to be taken into account. As a result the windscreen became more upright. Overhang at the front was increased by 2.8in (70mm) and the bonnet was lengthened and flattened; this squared up the front end from the noticeably softer proposal. Lack of time meant that sympathetic changes to the flat surfaces could not be made and maybe that is just as well. It is difficult to find a more cleanly executed contemporary front end.

Just two small details were changed before the final design was signed off; both were to do with saving production costs and both related to the lights. At the back the light clusters were shrunk, which Giugiaro felt was a big mistake as they started to look lost and visually 'wobbled'. When the Golf was given a facelift in 1981 he was much happier with the larger light housings, which were closer to the original design. At the front the proposed oblong headlamps were dumped on grounds of cost and replaced by off the shelf circular ones. This last change worried Giugiaro who felt that he was repeating himself after combining a rectangular grille and round headlights in the Giulia GT. Giugiaro can be credited with the innovative use of the full width grille and integral headlamps on the

Alfa Romeo Sprint, which finally separated the nose of the car from the bumpers and helped change frontal car design for ever. No one at the time drew any connection between the Alfa Giulia GT and the new Golf. Giugiaro even admits that the round headlamp and rectangular grille arrangement has become the single most important identifying feature of the Golf. Even so there was a last minute rethink about the position of the indicators. For a time they were going to sit at either end of the grille adjacent to the headlamps, but they were relocated in the bumpers.

But perhaps the most original Golf design feature was the hatchback tailgate, even though Volkswagen had incorporated a rear door in their 1969 prototypes. Giugiaro claimed to be having fun when he designed the rear of the car, but he must have been aware that the previous rear door had been an unsatisfactory and flimsy affair in need of proper definition. So he came up with a new design that wrapped around the side of the car. At a stroke the

production process was simplified as the sides were incorporated into the door itself. This is a feature that has subsequently been copied the world over.

CRITICAL ACCLAIM

Within the design community, the Golf triggered some extreme reactions and Roy Axe, a British designer who has worked for Chrysler and Rover, has summed it up perfectly: 'Its angular style was quite a shock; the old school designers were appalled. But the Golf was fresh and new and captured everyone's imagination.' Nigel Chapman, head of Automotive design at the Royal College of Art agreed: 'It is for me, the car of the Seventies and Eighties. It is a seminal design, that created the aesthetic for the modern hatchback.'

At Ford, Uwe Bahsen, their design chief responsible for the Ford Sierra, uttered the immortal line that the Golf represented the 'origami school of car design' and added, 'it

Volkswagen's biggest leap forward in thirty years. All they did was put a water cooled engine up front and a hatchback behind. Result: a legend.

is possible to produce a folded cardboard model of the Mark 1 Golf whereas you cannot make one of, say, a Sierra.' In spite of those comments Bahsen was a big fan of the Golf and was merely illustrating how different designers approach the problem of styling bodywork. He had a theory that Italian designers operated from a unique perspective as they had no central design school and were more influenced by architecture. In effect it was sculpture rather than graphics that was the overriding styling force.

Tom Karen, who founded Ogle Design, also observed that the design was seen as 'brutal', but picked up Giugiaro's unhappiness with the line just below the windscreen and the concave rear window surround, and turned them into positive distinguishing features. Karen argued that such flaws gave the car character. So the Golf looked right. It was fresh and futuristic, but what about the engineering?

LOOKS GOOD, GOES GOOD

Front wheel drive was nothing new. Citroen's Traction Avant in 1934 proved that the concept was a sound one, but ruined the company in the process. The Mini with its transversely mounted engine proved to be a packaging triumph and spawned a whole family of related vehicles. The closest in spirit to the Golf was the flawed 5-door Austin Maxi – but the execution and quality of the cars could not have been more different.

For a start, the new Golf was light and structurally rigid. New computer stressing techniques helped the designers to take full advantage of the front wheel drive layout. They were consequently able to save a considerable amount of weight as all the engine, suspension and braking stresses could be contained up front in a strong bulkhead. So the Golf weighed in at a remarkably light 1,700lb (772kg). Low fuel consumption was the effect, although there were no compromises in crash protection. At the heart of the new car's practicality was the transversely mounted engine set slightly ahead of the front wheel centreline. As a result interior space was generous, there was no intrusive transmission tunnel and the car had a large rear load area. The stubby front and rear styling only helped to make Golfs perfect to park.

Volkswagen could have got the next ingredient badly wrong. When it came to ancient air cooled technology there was not much that Volkswagen did not already know, but otherwise they were water cooled virgins. However, Volkswagen developed a very capable engine, which like the others in the Golf range was a belt driven, single overhead camshaft unit. This engine powered the base model displacing 1,093cc and producing 50bhp. It featured a crossflow cylinder head and was mounted at a 15-degree forward inclination. The bigger alternative was a 1,471cc engine producing 70hp and mounted with a 20-degree bias to the rear. This unit had last been seen in a longitudinal position underneath the bonnets of the Audi 80 and Passat, Volkswagen's first successful forays into water-cooled motoring. A 4-speed, all synchromesh gearbox or a 3-speed automatic mated exclusively to the bigger engine took care of the power, which was fed to the front wheels through drive shafts fitted with constant velocity joints.

If the engines turned out to be modern yet conventional, the real innovations could be found underneath where the chassis and suspension would confound the critics. At the front it seemed conventional enough with MacPherson struts supported by wishbones. Volkswagen modified the

Mark 1 Golf 1100L
Engine

Four cylinder in line, toothed belt driven SOHC
Alloy cylinder head, cast iron block transversely mounted in front

Capacity	1,093cc
Bore	69.5 × 72mm
Output	50bhp at 6000rpm
Compression ratio	8.0:1
Maximum torque	57lb/ft at 3000rpm

Transmission

Front wheel drive
4-speed all synchromesh

Suspension

Front	Independent with MacPherson struts, lower wishbones, coil springs
Rear	Semi-independent with trailing arms, torsion beam, coil springs, telescopic dampers

Steering

Rack and pinion
3.3 turns lock to lock

Brakes

9.4in (239mm) front discs, 8.9in (226mm) rear drums
Vacuum servo

Dimensions

Track – front	54.7in (1,389mm)
Track –rear	53in (1,346mm)
Wheelbase	94.5in (2,400mm)
Length	146.5in (3,721mm)
Width	63.5in (1,613mm)
Height	55.5in (1,410mm)
Ground clearance	5.3in (135mm)
Unladen weight	1,808lb (820.8kg)

Performance

Top speed	92mph (148kph)
Acceleration	0–60mph in 15.5 seconds

Fuel consumption

30.1mpg (9.3 litres per 100km)

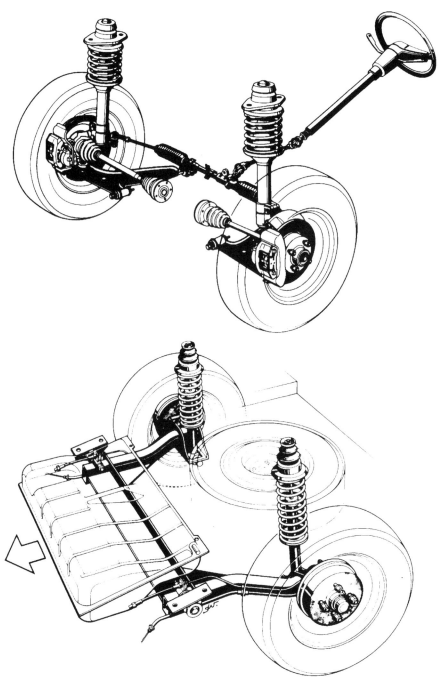

The secret of Golf's handling success. Basically it amounted to MacPherson struts at the front and torsion beam at the rear.

layout with state of the art bushes and an offset coil spring; low speed ride was no longer jerky like other MacPherson set-ups. In addition, negative offset steering – first seen on the Audi 80 and Passat – provided some self-correcting stability under braking if one side of the car was on a slippery surface, or there had been a puncture. At the back was a more complex though very clever independent suspension arrangement first seen on the Scirocco, which consisted of trailing arms, angled spring and damper units, plus a transverse member pivoted at its end on rubber bushes that linked backed to the trailing arms.

As well as cutting down the natural tendency of a front wheel drive car to understeer and increasing roll stiffness, the decision to locate the anti-roll bar solidly to the trailing arms was a crucial one. It removed many of the stresses affecting each arm that would otherwise have twisted them out of line, while the rear roll stiffness could be fine tuned with a strong yet flexible cross-beam. Basically it all added up to great handling.

LAUNCH

So the new Volkswagen looked good, drove well and handled brilliantly – the perfect package in fact. But the motoring press were still able to find some fault. The firm seating arrangements, especially the backrests, did not suit all tastes. Those differently angled drive shafts promoted torque steer under hard acceleration. Testers also reckoned that the steering was slightly under-geared. And when it came to using the Golf in anger, the brakes were not up to the job. The entry level 50bhp model had drums all round and the others featured solid discs at the front. Nit-picking aside, the Golf was an unqualified success and

GOLF OR GULF?

Have you ever wondered where the name Golf came from? Well, it is all to do with matters meteorological. The name is based on the Gulf Stream, which is responsible for Western Europe's moderate climate. In German gulf is spelt 'golf'. It all makes sense when you think about the other windy cars in the model line-up. The Scirocco is a hot wind, the Passat a warm one and the Jetta is a jet of air. In later years, Volkswagen sought to clear up any confusion over the spelling and the obvious fact that Golf is a game involving little white balls. Even the GTI and its golf ball topped gear stick (who said Germans have no sense of humour?) had reinforced the sport theme. The official explanation, which has lost something in the translation, went like this: 'Golf is the game and the name suits. Golf stands for endurance, perfect technique and – drive.'

the instant market leader in a niche that had not previously existed. All it needed now was customers.

Potential Golf buyers were first teased by the Scirocco at the 1974 Geneva Motor Show. This new coupé would act as the test bed for the forthcoming hatchback because the Scirocco shared the 94.5in (2,400mm) wheelbase, engines and virtually all the running gear. The idea was that if the specialist coachbuilders Karmann came across any teething troubles, they could overcome them quickly and quietly while operating at the low volume end of the market.

The wait was over by 1974 as the 3-door Golf entered production in July with the 5-door following in August. When the Golf finally reached the UK in October 1974 there were six versions on offer, a combination of 3 and 5-door models with 1.1 or 1.5 litre power units. Standard L trim was the

*A 1975 UK market
1.5 engined Golf.*

entry level, although a 5-door 1.5 LS was a class apart and came with plenty of extras. On the outside you could spot the difference because of the stainless steel window surrounds, door handles and strips of chrome that decorated the LS waistline. Inside the LS was much more luxurious. Gone was the golfer trouser check seat material, to be replaced by high quality one colour cloth. Those seats did not just look better, they even reclined. Drivers also had somewhere to rest their elbows, they were warmer thanks to a two speed heater blower, much better informed because of the extra instrumentation (rev counter), able to smoke because of the cigarette lighter, more secure due to the lockable glove compartment and less bothered by engine and road noise as a result of additional insulation material.

In the load bay there was a cover, and pneumatic tailgate arms made opening the tailgate easy. The LS got a major engine upgrade in September 1975 when the cylinder bore was increased from 76.5 to 79.5mm, raising the capacity from 1,471 to 1,588cc. Minor changes involved ditching the oddments tray mounted over the trans-

mission tunnel and installing a proper central console with integral clock. However, that 1,588cc engine was soon to be installed in a much more potent state of tune.

The three most important letters in the history of the Golf were fused in 1976 with the announcement of the remarkable GTI. Even so, in 1976 after that long sweltering summer the only way you could get your hands on one of these fuel injected, 1,588cc engined screamers was to place a special order at your local dealer and even then it would be left hand drive. UK buyers had to wait until March 1979 before they could officially place an order for a right hand drive example.

Back among the high specification LS models, a brand new 1,457cc engine with the larger 79.5mm bore and shorter 73.4mm stroke was installed from September 1978. It was also used to power another more comprehensively equipped GLS model, basically an LS with a few more features, including bronze-tinted glass, chrome hub caps, higher quality upholstery and a brushed aluminium dashboard with a raft of additions and improvements. These upgrades included rheostat illumination, a water temperature gauge, a quartz clock and a padded steering wheel, which all improved the driver's outlook and comfort. The GLS package was briefly available at this time with the 1.1 engine.

That smaller engine formed the basis for another unit in September 1979 when it was bored out to 75mm – the resulting

---

Mark 1 Golf Diesel (LD)

Engine

	Four cylinder in line, toothed belt driven SOHC
	Alloy cylinder head, cast iron block transversely mounted in front
Capacity	1,471cc
Bore	80.0 × 76.5mm
Output	50bhp at 5000rpm
Compression ratio	23.5:1
Maximum torque	56.5lb/ft at 3000rpm

Transmission

	Front wheel drive
	4-speed all synchromesh

Suspension

Front	Independent with MacPherson struts, lower wishbones, coil springs
Rear	Semi-independent with trailing arms, torsion beam, coil springs, telescopic dampers

Steering

	Rack and pinion
	3.3 turns lock to lock

Brakes

	9.4in (239mm) front discs, 8.9in (226mm) rear drums
	Vacuum servo

Dimensions

Track – front	54.7in (1,389mm)
Track – rear	53in (1,346mm)
Wheelbase	94.5in (2,400mm)
Length	146.5in (3,721mm)
Width	63.5in (1,613mm)
Height	55.5in (1,410mm)
Ground clearance	5.3in (135mm)
Unladen weight	1,918lb (870.8kg)

Performance

Top speed	85mph (137kph)
Acceleration	0–60mph in 15.5 seconds

Fuel consumption

	46.0mpg (6.1 litres per 100km)

Volkswagen proved with the Golf that diesels do not have to be boring. Here is a European specification GTD, a diesel with all the usual GTI trimmings.

1,272cc produced 60bhp. The original 1,471cc engine was used for the first diesel model to make it to the UK in April 1978, badged as the LD, with LS specification plus a cold-start button. For a diesel, it delivered remarkable levels of refinement and speed and proved that this sort of frugal unit could be used effectively in something other than truck or a taxi. Fuel economy was excellent at 62.6mpg (4.5 litres per 100km) at a constant 50mph (80kph) and the engine could match the 1.1 litre petrol unit for output and performance, as both could top 87mph (140kph). At the time even Motor commented that 'it could easily be mistaken for a petrol engined car'. So began our acceptance of the oil-burning hatchback.

Stylistically not much had happened to the Golf since its launch, but there was a mild facelift for the 1980 model year. At the front there were brand new wrap-around bumpers. The matt black era was upon us and the previous chrome inserts were condemned. At the back, there were more wrap-around bumpers plus significantly enlarged rear light clusters, and the GL and GLS got wider strips of trim around the waistline.

In June 1979, Volkswagen introduced one of their most popular and enduring special editions, the Golf Driver. Essentially this was a GTI without any performance hassles, a sheep in wolfish clothing. The marketing department mixed and matched the specification and used as their starting point a 3-door model with 1.3 engine and 4-speed gearbox. To this they added GTI side stripes, black rear light cluster panels and bigger 5.5J × 13in wheels with 175/70SR-13 tyres. On the inside a GL dashboard and centre console featured a clock and voltmeter. Sports seats and steering wheel looked and felt the part, and a passenger side storage shelf and door pockets were welcome practical additions. As well as the black velour carpets the whole GTI effect was topped off with a golf ball shaped gear knob. All the customer had to do was choose between red, orange and green paintwork. The good old diesel still managed to chug along reliably, modified in line with the petrol N and L models. However, in September 1980 it too benefited from the bigger 79.5 × 80mm 1,588cc engine.

RE-STYLED INTERIOR

In July 1981 the interior was re-vamped. The biggest improvement was to the dashboard as the instruments were grouped behind a non reflective panel. Ventilation was improved with the addition of ventilation outlets in central and side positions and an attractive new safety feature was a range of padded steering wheels. It was

also time to overhaul the nomenclature so it was all change on the badge front. The new line-up comprised C, C Diesel, CL, GL and GTI. The C replaced the base N, and now had halogen headlamps, swivel sun visors, new trim materials and moulded rear seats. Likewise the CL was a direct replacement for the LS, which meant some bright work around the screen and window surrounds, a digital clock, lockable glove box and intermittent wash/wipe. Meanwhile the GLS became the GL with top of the range trim, hub caps and headlamp washers.

September 1981 was also when penny pinchers could save a little fuel provided they stuck with the high compression 1,093cc engine and could bear the Formel E designation. What you got for your extra money was a high ratio 3+E (economy) gearbox with ratios of 3.45, 1.77. 1.054 and 0.8:1. The fourth gear was an overdrive that dropped the revs down by about 1000rpm when engaged. More exciting was a combined fuel consumption and gear change indicator that flashed a red light at you when it was time to change up and encouraged you to keep the needle in the frugal area of 45mpg (6.2 litres per 100km) or better. There were also the GTI-like windscreen pillar deflectors and a larger front spoiler.

The first facelift – more matt black plastic. The bigger rear light clusters were much more to Giugiaro's liking.

A 1981 Golf Driver, one of the most enduringly popular variations on the Golf theme, which aped the GTI in appearance rather than performance.

MARK 1 SPECIALS

By 1983 the Golf was just months away from replacement by an all new model. In common with all other manufacturers faced with the predicament of selling their last few cars and making them even more attractive to buyers, the marketing department at Volkswagen came up with two special editions. The Driver was a return to the successful clone GTI formula first used in 1980. This time based on the humble 3-door C, it looked even more like the hottest hatchback with the adoption of the distinctive four headlamp grille from the GTI. In addition the black wheel arch mouldings, side stripes and passenger door mirror completed the bodywork transformation. Sports seats, a tachometer, digital clock and centre console were enough to make a real GTI driver double take.

The other special edition also took some GTI cues. Based on the 1.5 GL, the GX was virtually a Driver for the more mature owner and had five doors. Outside were the four headlamp grille, wider 5J × 13in wheels (with hub caps) and 175/70SR-13 tyres and chrome embellishment around the grille, windows and body trim. The sports front seats, centre console, tachometer, lockable glove box and full carpeting made the GX a comfortable place to be.

END OF THE LINE

The Mark 1 Golf ceased production in the summer of 1983 and although most models were deleted in July of that year, the GL was still listed in the UK market until January 1984. The figures were impressive – six million Golfs had found homes throughout the world and the customers were not disappointed. The Golf was an important model – the car of the decade – and had caught a lot of manufacturers napping. Suddenly they had a lot of catching up to do. The Japanese in particular had taken the Golf lessons to heart. They appreciated the value of good build quality, versatile hatchback body styles and a common front wheel drive platform that could accommodate a whole range of related models. Nissan, Mitsubishi and Honda apparently all bought brand new Golfs so that they could learn more about this new type of car. A glance at the Honda Accord and Prelude range introduced in 1976 indicates that the company were taking lots of design and product planning lessons on board. Credit must go in part to the Golf for helping spearhead the Japanese invasions of the European hatchback and American compact markets.

Volkswagen had well and truly replaced the Beetle and the company was poised to update their second most successful model. Unfortunately, Giugiaro was not going to be around to do it. The Volkswagen revival can be credited almost solely to Giugiaro who within months had re-vamped Volkswagen's entire range by designing three seminal models: the revolutionary Golf, capable Passat and beautiful Scirocco. Because (with the exception of the Passat) the gestation period was so short, the original design concept stayed pure. The Golf in particular was one man's vision with the minimum of interference from marketing, the board of directors, or

This 1982 Open Air Golf now lives in the Volkswagen museum, the best place for the beachy, doorless vehicle, designed to tow trailers full of tourists around. It is automatic and has extremely large rear view mirrors.

A 1985 proposal from Volkswagen in the UK was this Golf Caddy Sport. Under the bonnet was a GTI engine, while the ride height was raised, a body kit was added along with alloy wheels and all manner of roof and roll bars.

customer clinics to dilute the original concept. Kurt Lotz, who had been wise enough to sign up the designer so quickly in 1969, had wanted to go even further and retain Giugiaro's services for future projects. New man at the top Rudolf Leidling disagreed, so when it came to design the next generation of Golfs, Volkswagen were on their own.

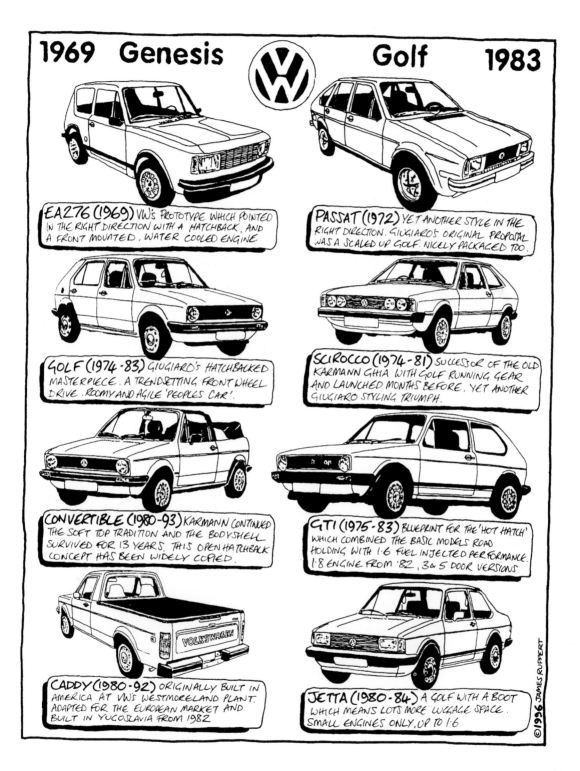

1969 Genesis Golf 1983

EA276 (1969) VW's PROTOTYPE WHICH POINTED IN THE RIGHT DIRECTION WITH A HATCHBACK, AND A FRONT MOUNTED, WATER COOLED ENGINE

PASSAT (1972) YET ANOTHER STYLE IN THE RIGHT DIRECTION. GIUGIARO'S ORIGINAL PROPOSAL WAS A SCALED UP GOLF. NICELY PACKAGED TOO.

GOLF (1974-83) GIUGIARO'S HATCHBACKED MASTERPIECE. A TRENDSETTING FRONT WHEEL DRIVE. ROOMY AND AGILE 'PEOPLES CAR'.

SCIROCCO (1974-81) SUCCESSOR OF THE OLD KARMANN GHIA WITH GOLF RUNNING GEAR AND LAUNCHED MONTHS BEFORE. YET ANOTHER GIUGIARO STYLING TRIUMPH.

CONVERTIBLE (1980-93) KARMANN CONTINUED THE SOFT TOP TRADITION AND THE BODYSHELL SURVIVED FOR 13 YEARS. THIS OPEN HATCHBACK CONCEPT HAS BEEN WIDELY COPIED.

GTI (1975-83) BLUEPRINT FOR THE 'HOT HATCH' WHICH COMBINED THE BASIC MODELS ROAD HOLDING WITH 1·6 FUEL INJECTED PERFORMANCE. 1·8 ENGINE FROM '82, 3 & 5 DOOR VERSIONS

CADDY (1980-92) ORIGINALLY BUILT IN AMERICA AT VW'S WESTMORELAND PLANT. ADAPTED FOR THE EUROPEAN MARKET AND BUILT IN YUGOSLAVIA FROM 1982

JETTA (1980-84) A GOLF WITH A BOOT WHICH MEANS LOTS MORE LUGGAGE SPACE. SMALL ENGINES ONLY, UP TO 1·6

©1996 JAMES RUPPERT

39

3   The Hatchback Gets Hot

'A tiger in a three piece suit' – *Motor Trend.*

We have the GTI to enjoy today because a small group of Volkswagen engineers decided to put hundreds of hours of unpaid overtime into a prototype Golf. In March 1973 work began on the prototype code numbered EA337, which would eventually become the Mark 1 Golf. The credit goes not to the marketing department but to this handful of engineers with more than a passing interest in motor racing. They eventually built six prototypes and set about proving that Volkswagen's new car could more than handle an extra turn of speed. Such an unusual and unofficial development programme obviously contributed to the purity and quality of the final product, but outside this enthusiastic circle of engineers it proved hard to find any other Sport Golf fans.

Credit for the GTI concept ought to go to Dr Friedrich Goes. He knew his way around the Audi-Volkswagen parts bin and came up with the Audi engine, wider tyres

Inside one of the first GTIs. You are not meant to snigger at the plaid seats, but you may allow yourself a titter at the gear knob. Yes, it really is a golf ball, painted black.

First appearance of the 'Sport Golf' in August 1975 just before the Frankfurt Motor show. In prototype form the badges have a different typeface, a small front spoiler and a rear plate panel with a flanged pressing that would be changed before production.

and a suspension system that was stiffened, lowered and beefed up with an anti-roll bar. Inside the original prototype there was also a set of Recaro sports seats. Apparently he was told to park the prototype in the basement and forget all about it. The next time he heard about the Sporting Golf he was working for Volkswagen in America and it had become the GTI. (Goes put his mix and match engineering talents to good use when in the 1990s he helped to assemble the new Seat Ibiza. The model that attracted the most attention was the Ibiza GTi, which had Volkswagen's 2.0 litre engine and coincidentally benefited from Giugiaro-styled bodywork. The GTI has been effectively reborn in Spain, but in 1973 the future for the Sport Golf looked bleak.)

When the project was revealed to senior management, they did not initially see the positive side. Volkswagen had a mass market hatchback to shift and a whole company to save from sliding sales and impending bankruptcy. Even the sales department could not see a market for a performance version of the new car. Such attitudes were hardly surprising. After all, with manufacturers like Alfa Romeo, BMW and Jaguar, which have a sporting pedigree, customers expect sports car speed, handling and excitement from their saloons as well as the dedicated sports models. But from the company that brought you the Beetle, all a Volkswagen buyer would ever expect is that it would start first time and never break down.

There were few precedents for taking production models and hotting them up for anything other purely cynical marketing purposes. A go faster stripe here and an extra carburettor there was all any transformation really amounted to. Mass market rivals Ford had a similar image problem to Volkswagen – being associated with dull but worthy family cars – but they significantly changed their image by linking up with Lotus to produce a performance version of the Cortina. Across their range this resulted in the RS (Rally Sport) abbreviation becoming synonymous with powerful Ford sports saloons.

An original GTI doing what it did best, transforming the staid image of Volkswagen – GTI as an automatic icon.

COOPER CONNECTION

Perhaps the most direct spiritual predecessor was the Mini Cooper. Like the Golf, the front wheel drive Mini was born as a fully formed motor car that was perfect right from the start. Early versions of the Mini quickly proved that they had incredibly good handling and could easily cope with increased power. The Volkswagen engineers and ultimately the sales department were starting to get the same message. The Golf proved to be similar to the Mini in so many ways. Both were cleverly packaged, classless, ground breaking designs that revolutionized the way cars were made.

Each set the tone for its respective decade, spawned dozens of imitators and redefined what a sports car could be: practical, economical and fun without a hint of compromise.

However, the engineers did not know that they had an iconoclastic vehicle on their hands, even though the EA337 was the ideal basis for a performance car. It was light yet immensely strong, with agile suspension featuring MacPherson struts up front and a torsion beam at the rear, even if the brakes would only ever be adequate. Nevertheless with encouraging driver feedback and a less sceptical sales department, the Sport Golf was officially sanctioned in

---

GTI DEFINED

The origins of the best known performance cachet in motoring is lost in Volkswagen myth and legend. Certainly 'Gran Turismo' was always accepted as a designation for some the world's finest specialist sports cars, like the Aston Martin DB4 GT Zagato. Over the years though, those two innocent letters were appropriated by marketing departments and glued onto any dull model that needed a sales boost. Volkswagen were aware that the letters had been debased and sought to distinguish their new sports model by adding 'I' for fuel injection.

It has been suggested that as the German for fuel injection is 'Einspritzung' the designation GTE should have been used, as on its subsequent rival the Vauxhall Astra. But Audi had already used GTE for an 80 model so it was decided to distinguish the Volkswagen and opt for I for injection. BMW had already set a precedent with its use on their Bosch-injected CSi coupés. However,

Volkswagen set themselves apart by using a capital I – except in South Africa where the designation was GTi – and their only regret must be not having patented those three precious letters as a trademark to prevent everyone else from jumping on the bandwagon.

The GTI badge on a Mark 2 Golf.

May 1975, just a year after the Golf had entered production. Herbert Schuster was transferred from Audi to co-ordinate the new project, which was now known as the GTI.

THE FIRST FIVE THOUSAND

By the time Volkswagen had embraced this new model, almost all the serious development work had been done, which was a good thing as there was not much time. Even so, fifteen durability models carried out the usual programme of rigorous testing – cars were sent north to Scandinavia for winter trials and south to Africa to see how they performed at the other extreme. Internally there was plenty of debate over how the new model should be packaged. A stripped out, no frills, no nonsense GTI aimed at purely young enthusiasts was a favoured option for a time. However, for the older and more affluent driver such a model would not be so attractive, so it was decided to fit what was by German standards a high level of equipment and trim. When it was launched however, the model turned out to be distinctively subtle, Spartan even, and true to the engineers' original intentions – thanks in part to last minute financial jitters as the company tried to keep costs within reasonable bounds.

Approval was given for a limited production run of 5,000, which was the minimum number required to qualify the car for competition purposes. A prototype was first exhibited at the 1975 Frankfurt Motor Show and nine months later the GTI was in full production.

At the heart of the high performance Golf was an engine that had first seen service in the Audi 80 GT. The original 1,471cc unit was bored out from 76.5 to 79.5mm and the result was a 1,588cc capacity. In addition it had larger diameter inlet valves with Heron-type combustion chambers, while the gas flow was improved by revised inlet and exhaust manifolds. Early prototypes ran with a twin-choke Solex carburettor with a 9.7:1 compression ratio and managed to squeeze 100bhp at 6,000rpm. However, Volkswagen went for another rummage around their parts bin and came up with a Bosch K-Jetronic fuel injection system that had first been used in the American market to make the Audi 80 and Volkswagen Passat comply with emission regulations. This modification conjured up an extra 10bhp, and the compression ratio was lowered to 9.5:1.

Apart from the engine, other modifications that set the GTI apart were an oil cooler, oil temperature gauge and tachometer. Power was delivered through a larger clutch to a standard gearbox, although the final drive ratio was changed from 3.9:1 to 3.7:1. Keeping it on the road were specially rated Bilstein shock absorbers backed up

GTI 1600

Engine

Four cylinder in line, toothed belt driven SOHC
Alloy cylinder head, cast iron block transversely mounted in front

Bosch K-Jetronic fuel injection

Capacity	1,588cc
Bore	79.5 × 80mm
Output	110bhp at 6100rpm
Compression ratio	9.5:1
Maximum torque	102.9lb/ft at 5000rpm

Transmission

Front wheel drive

4-speed all synchromesh	3.45, 1.94, 1.37, 0.97:1
Reverse	3.17:1
Final drive	3.7:1
5-speed	3.45, 2.12, 1.44, 1.13, 0.91:1
Reverse	3.17:1
Final drive	3.9:1

Suspension

Front	Independent with MacPherson struts, lower wishbones, coil springs and anti-roll bar
Rear	Semi-independent with trailing arms, torsion beam, coil springs, telescopic dampers and anti-roll bar

Steering

Rack and pinion
3.3 turns lock to lock

Brakes

9.4in (239mm) ventilated front discs, 8.9in (226mm) rear drums
Vacuum servo

Tyres and wheels

175/70HR-13 on 5.5J × 13

Dimensions

Track – front	55.3in (1,405mm)
Track – rear	54in (1,372mm)
Wheelbase	94.5in (2,400mm)
Length	150.2in (3,815mm)
Width	64.1in (1,628mm)
Height	54.9in (1,394mm)
Unladen weight	1,850lb (840kg)

Performance

Top speed	112mph (180kph)
Acceleration	0–60mph in 9.1 seconds

Fuel consumption

Urban	26.9mpg (10.5 litres per 100km)
Constant 56mph (90kph)	38.2mpg (7.4 litres per 100km)
Constant 75mph (121kph)	29.7mpg (9.5 litres per 100km)

The first in a long line of Golfs to wear the discreet GTI badging.

by anti-roll bars all round. The suspension itself remained at the original ride height, but it was soon lowered by 0.8in (20mm) – which not only looked good but meant better handling. Doing the gripping was a set of 175/70HR-13 tyres attached to 5.5in wheel rims. Ventilated disc brakes at the front backed up by a larger servo brought the car to a halt.

Perhaps the most attractive aspect of this new Golf was its understated looks. Volkswagen kept the go faster trimmings to a minimum. Apart from the subtly lower ride height, spoked sports wheels, chunkier spoiler, plastic wheel arch surrounds (a feature that designer Giugiaro always hated, but recognized was a necessary compromise of mass production), side strip above the sill and discreet badging there were few other clues that this Golf was anything special. The sports seats with hideous tartan facings hinted that this was a far from standard Golf. Drivers could have fun with the three-spoke sports steering wheel, centre console and hilarious golf ball topped gear stick.

HOT HATCH, COLD RIVALS

That first modest target of 5,000 was soon exceeded and production was running at

5,000 per month. It arrived in a deserted auto universe where there was no direct competition. In a road test in December 1976, *Motor* judged the principal GTI rivals to be the Ford Escort RS2000, Triumph Dolomite Sprint, Renault 17TS, Colt Galant GTO and Alfa Romeo Alfetta 1.8. This was a strange bunch, and some saloons were tossed in for variety, but there was nothing that came close in style or execution. The Renault did have a rear door and front wheel drive, yet it was little more than a good old fashioned fastback coupé with average performance and bizarre styling. The Golf on the other hand was viewed as a homologation special (made in sufficient quantities for the model to be considered eligible for production car racing).

The magazine article observed: 'If done well – and the GTI has been done very well indeed – the result is not only suitable for competition, but also a taut high performance car entirely acceptable to the ordinary driver with sporting tastes.' They liked the handling, but not as much as the Alfetta. They thought that for its size the accommodation was excellent and went overboard about the quietness and overall refinement. The performance was off Volkswagen's official pace, but that particular press fleet car, MKT 512R, always produced disappointing figures. *Motor* also noticed that the gear lever top was shaped like a golf ball, 'but coloured black'.

LEFT HAND DRIVE ONLY

As much as the UK press raved about the new model, there was a problem. Introduced in October 1976, the GTI was available to special order only in left hand drive. Volkswagen had not even anticipated such a huge overseas demand and for the time being could not keep all their cus-

tomers happy. Nevertheless specialist companies, GTI Engineering in particular, would carry out right hand drive conversions to a very high standard. Patient UK buyers had to wait until July 1979 before they could order an officially imported right hand drive GTI.

When they did arrive the right hand drive models looked much better, as during 1978 the slender girder type bumpers were replaced by more substantial plastic wrap-around versions that extended to the wheel arches. January 1980 heralded the

Revised fascia on the 1981 cars set the design tone for GTI and Golf interiors thereafter. Inside, everything is in sight and within reach. This is a 1983 Campaign model.

welcome arrival of a 5-speed gearbox. Although Volkswagen had introduced a similar gearbox into the American market the previous year, the ratios for the GTI were to be much closer at 3.45, 2.118, 1.444, 1.129 and 0.912:1. This meant that there was a noticeable improvement in acceleration: the 0–60mph time dropped down to 8.5 seconds and the top speed climbed a little to 113mph (182kph). To make the GTI just that bit more desirable new alloy wheels were standard.

September now took on a special significance for the GTI as changes were made every subsequent season. For the 1981 model year the fascia was redesigned. It set the pattern for Golf instrumentation into the 1990s, as the speedometer and rev counter were positioned under non reflective plastic rather than in separate bezels and were joined by a digital clock, with a grouping of ten warning lights above it. In front of the binnacle was a new four-spoke padded steering wheel. The centre console was revised and like the rest of the range ventilation was improved with extra fresh air vents positioned above a revised centre console. There was even more storage space on the passenger side of the fascia. To everyone's relief the gaudy checked upholstery was replaced by more subtle striped trim.

FRENCH CONNECTION

By the early 1980s it was noticeable that other manufacturers were copying the hot hatch concept very successfully and were starting to tempt customers away from the GTI. What the Golf needed to do was take a quantum leap ahead of the pack and Volkswagen France reckoned it could be done. They already felt threatened by the Fiat Abarth Ritmo and Renault Alpine in particular. Their radical response was to fit

an engine tuned by Oettinger. This was a 16-valve conversion producing 136bhp and the model was badged as the Golf GTI 16S. The rest of the specification included a full width air dam, 6J × 14in alloy wheels, extended wheel arches and sills, plus a twin headlamp grille. Inside there were more instruments and a 16S decal on the steering wheel. The choice of colour was white or metallic black. Top speed was claimed as 122mph (196kph) and it sold in France for the equivalent of £6,800.

An internal memo in June 1981 recommended that the 16S should be seriously considered by Volkswagen in the UK. The only drawback was an £8,000 retail price, but it was reckoned that it would be possible to sell at least 200 by marketing it as an exclusive, restricted production performance Golf that would maintain interest in the GTI as a whole, while being extremely profitable. Unfortunately, no action was taken.

FURTHER REFINEMENT

For the 1982 model year the GTI got further aerodynamic assistance, courtesy of windscreen pillar air deflectors. At the back, the rear light clusters grew a little and joined up with the registration plate. On the inside the door pulls were repositioned at a more rakish angle; below them were new door pockets and loudspeaker pods.

In September 1982 the good news was the installation of a 1,800cc engine. This 1,781cc unit was a 1600 bored out from 79.5 to 81mm and with an increased stroke, 86.4mm up from 80mm. But the good news did not end there. Pistons, connecting rods and several other moving items were lightened. The valve size increased and the cylinder head was

Golf GTI 16S for France only – the Oettinger tuned model had a 16-valve cylinder several years before the factory officially fitted one.

49

It looked the same on the outside, but underneath the bonnet was a usefully bigger 1.8 litre unit, which boosted performance and flexibility.

modified. The compression ratio therefore went up to 10:1 – mid range torque was improved and alterations were made to the valve timing. As a result peak torque (109lb/ft) was achieved at 3,500rpm and maximum 112bhp power delivered at 5,800rpm. In addition a new crankshaft was fitted with a torsional vibration damper.

The GTI borrowed a useful little gadget from the Formel E, an economy gauge and gear change indicator, so it was not just quick, but frugal too. A temperature gauge was added to the instrument pack, but perhaps the most novel provider of informa-tion was the MFA on-board computer. Operated by pressing a button on the end of the windscreen wiper stalk, an LED dis-play at the bottom of the binnacle showed the distance travelled and the fuel con-sumption. It is probably the most brilliant-ly simple device of its kind ever fitted to a car.

The arrival of the larger power unit proved an opportune time for the motoring press to compare the increasing number of hot hatch rivals that aped and attempted to overtake the original GTI. Motor tested the bigger engined models just weeks before the arrival of the injected Vauxhall

GTI 1800

Engine

Four cylinder in line, toothed belt driven SOHC
Alloy cylinder head, cast iron block transversely mounted in front
Bosch K-Jetronic fuel injection

Capacity 1,781cc
Bore 81× 86.4mm
Output 112bhp at 5800rpm
Compression ratio 10.0:1
Maximum torque 109lb/ft at 3500rpm

Transmission

Front wheel drive 3.45, 2.12, 1.44, 1.13, 0.91:1
Reverse 3.17:1
Final drive 3.65:1

Suspension

Front Independent with MacPherson struts, lower wishbones, coil springs and anti-roll bar
Rear Semi-independent with trailing arms, torsion beam, coil springs, telescopic dampers and anti-roll bar

Steering

Rack and pinion
3.3 turns lock to lock

Brakes

9.4in (239mm) ventilated front discs, 8.9in (226mm) rear drums
Vacuum servo

Tyres and wheels

175/70HR-13 on 5.5J × 13

Dimensions

Track – front 55.3in (1,405mm)
Track – rear 54in (1,372mm)
Wheelbase 94.5in (2,400mm)
Length 150.2in (3,815mm)
Width 64.1in (1,628mm)
Height 54.9in (1,394mm)
Unladen weight 1,850lb (840kg)

Performance

Top speed 114mph (183kph)
Acceleration 0–60mph in 8.2 seconds

Fuel consumption

Urban	26.6mpg (10.6 litres per 100km)
Constant 56mph (90kph)	47.9mpg (5.9 litres per 100km)
Constant 75mph (121kph)	36.7mpg (7.7 litres per 100km)

The Mark 1 GTI: a neat design classic that set performance car standards other manufactures had to try and match.

Astra GTE and Ford Escort XR3i. Also considered was the charisma free Volvo 360 GLT, hatchback Alfasud TiX, rapidly improving Renault Gordini Turbo and outclassed Fiat Strada 105 TC. They loved the gear ratios of the Golf 1.8 GTI, the power to weight ratio and above all the free revving and smooth engine that was more refined and quieter than the old 1.6. Like before, the handling was perfect and the brakes hardly inspired confidence. Although an all new model was only a year away, *Motor* could reach only one conclusion: 'the GTi still rules'.

The very last, special edition Mark 1 GTI was introduced in August 1983. Just 1,000 Campaigns were destined for the UK and were immediately recognizable because of the four headlamp grille and Pirelli 6J × 14in alloy wheels with 'P' cutouts, shod with 185/60HR-14 tyres. The standard equipment included a sunroof, tinted glass, metallic paint and a leather covered steering wheel. How on earth could Volkswagen top this?

Before the GTI, car buyers got by with traditional sports cars, sad old coupés and the occasional warmed up GT badged saloon. Just as the Golf reinvented the hatchback, so the GTI changed the way fast cars were designed and marketed. The GTI killed off a generation of inadequate, outdated sports cars and replaced them with a practical, affordable and fun-filled alternative. After the GTI, performance cars would never be the same again.

4 Bigger and Better – Golf Mark 2

'The Golf must remain a Golf' – Herbert Schäfer, head of the design department.

Wolfsburg had a problem. How do you replace the Golf? You do not tinker with a winning formula. Volkswagen had never changed any model simply for sake of it – witness the Beetle. Nevertheless they always developed their cars carefully and for the better. The automotive world was itself changing rapidly and in particular there were threats from Japan, where product cycles got shorter and shorter. In Europe too, other manufacturers had cottoned on to the hatchback concept. As a result, there was not going to be an equivalent quantum leap that took them from the old fashioned Beetle to the Golf Mark 1. That was not necessary – they beefed up the original concept.

NEW GOLF TAKES SHAPE

Work started on the Mark 2 as early as March 1977. Volkswagen commissioned freelance stylists as well as briefing in-house teams so that by November 1978 there were ten concepts to choose from. These were whittled down to two, which where refined until May 1979 when Volkswagen management opted for the in-house version. Later that year they had mules up and running to test new mechanical assemblies. Road going prototypes started work in May 1980.

In all, 49 cars were built for general testing and another 38 body shells for specific tests. Crash testing took care of 15 vehicles after their original tests were completed and 22 were dispatched for long distance road trials. These were later joined in February 1983 by cars from the initial pre-production batch of 300. Half went to the Volkswagen proving ground in Ehra-Lessien. More than 3.7 million miles (6 million kilometres) were covered by prototypes and test cars.

GOLF REMAINS THE SAME

The last thing that Volkswagen wanted to do was frighten off loyal customers. To complete Herr Schäfer's quote at the start of this chapter: 'Therefore the new Golf will inherit the unmistakable look of the Golf I with its typical shape.' For the styling they stuck with the most distinctive design cue and carried over the huge C pillar blind spot. In fact it got even bigger, so rearward three quarter vision was still something of a guessing game. To accommodate customers who were statistically getting larger and demanding increased accommodation, the new Golf grew up accordingly. The wheelbase was lengthened by 3in (75mm), the track by 0.9in (23mm) at the front and 2in (50mm) at the rear, while the overall length increased by 6.7in (170mm) and the

Prototypes were knocked into – and in some cases very much out of – shape as they were tested on the track, in the laboratory and way out in the desert to make sure that the Mark 2 was up to the Volkswagen standard.

Inside the Volkswagen design studio the interior and exterior of the new Mark 2 took shape.

width 2.2in (55mm). This meant a lot more room inside for passengers. Drivers found that there was a useful 1.5in (37mm) between the accelerator pedal and their seat and 3.7in (92mm) of additional elbow room. At the back, passengers' elbows had a massive 4.8in (120mm) more to play with and 3in (75mm) extra leg room, although the driver's seat had no more rear travel than before.

It is hardly surprising that the new Golf also piled on the weight, which went up from 1,850lb (840kg) to 2,026lb (920kg). It hardly made the Mark 2 sluggish, though, thanks to a dramatic improvement in the drag coefficient, up 19 per cent from 0.42 to 0.34. Making the Golf more slippery involved integrating the roof gutter into

Here is how Volkswagen altered Giugiaro's classic shape in three easy stages, making it longer, higher, wider and more rounded in the interests of aerodynamics, interior space and safety.

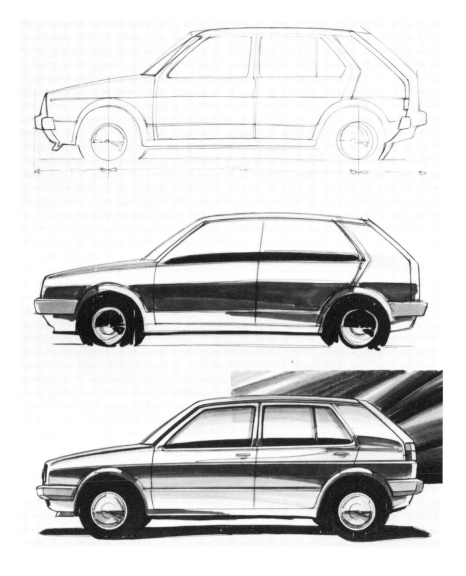

the panel itself, virtually flush door glass and softer, more rounded bodywork. All this helped to increase top speeds across the range by a little and to keep the wind noise down.

One of the strongest selling points of the old Golf had been build quality. Wolfsburg were in no mood to compromise in this area and rightly continued a long tradition of over-engineering their products. They had

even constructed a massive two-level assembly plant to cope with the projected increase in demand. There were automated production improvements (new robots), and innovations included dipping pre-heated body shells into liquid wax for maximum protection against corrosion.

Passengers in the Mark 2 felt the benefit of improved ventilation. A feature of the redesigned fascia was the twin air vents.

Hall 54, the new plant where Mark 2 Golfs were built from 1983. At the time it was one of the most advanced and automated production facilities of its kind.

This is the automated production line for the Mark 2 Golf.

The millionth Mark 2 Golf appeared in 1985.

This, combined with the much more efficient heater and additional floor mounted vents for rear passengers in GL and GTI models, made the Golf more comfortable in all climates.

Apart from those noticeable interior and exterior changes, the Mark 2 was mechanically very similar to the original Golf. This was due in part to Volkswagen's policy of test bedding components late in the life of their models, so that the 1982 Golf Mark 1 was in essence mechanically identical to the new Golfs launched in 1984. However, the new bodywork gave the company the opportunity to rework minor components and, most significantly, adjust the suspension settings. Ride quality was improved by giving the front suspension struts an extra 1in (25mm) of travel and the rear was increased by 0.4in (12mm).

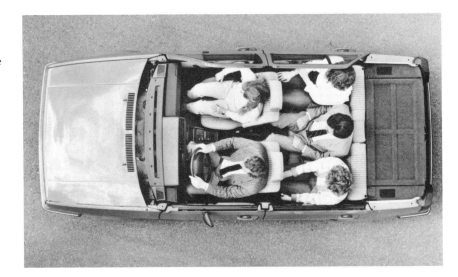

This ultimate Golf convertible is actually a launch demonstration of the amazing roominess of the Mark 2.

Inside a European specification Mark 2 the driver's view looked like this.

LAUNCH LINE-UP

The new range of Golfs came to the UK market in February 1984. A very basic entry level 1,043cc lasted only until July, hardly surprising as it was very under-powered with a Polo engine tuned to 45bhp pulling it along. Much better was the 3-door 1.3 C with rear wash/wipe and cloth door trims. A 5-speed, 5-door Formel E version was introduced at this time for the economy conscious. The 5-door CL featured additional twin fresh air vents, front door storage bins, a trip meter and centre console. The 5-door GL was now powered by the 1,595cc, 75bhp unit used in the con-

vertible version. A 4+E gearbox was standard, along with a split rear seat, metallic paint, body side rubbing strips and up market tweed upholstery. Topping the range was the GTI.

As usual, the diesel version had not quite caught up with the rest of the models and was launched a month later. Badged as a C and with the same specification as its petrol relatives, it retained the 1,588cc, 54bhp unit combined with the economy gearbox. More exciting was the introduction in January 1985 of a turbo diesel version. This produced a respectable 69bhp and was equipped to CL standard.

Limited edition fans did not have to wait

The Mark 2 Golf as introduced to the UK market in 5-door GL trim.

too long, as the Match was launched in May 1985. Based on the 1.3 CL it came with the GTI type four headlamp grille and white colour coding on the bumpers, door mirrors and wheels. The all white theme continued inside with white seats (plus tasteful black stripes) and carpets. The saving grace was useful split rear seats, a centre console, quartz clock, sports steering wheel and comfortable sports seats.

NO QUARTER, PROPER WIPER

Range revisions began in September 1985 when the base C model benefited from electronic ignition, side indicators and flat faced hub caps. The CFE was replaced by the CL, the 4+E gearbox becoming an option. In addition to the C upgrades and side indicators the CL interior gained door pockets, a centre console and Alpine tweed trim, which was not as exotic as it sounded. The 1.6 GL was replaced by a CL equipped as the 1.3 but with the economy gearbox as standard. The most important new model was the 1.8 GL, with a 1,781cc, 90bhp engine that was closely related to the GTI units except that there was a carburettor instead of petrol injection. Specification was as CL plus chrome window surrounds, internally adjustable mirrors, tachometer and front head restraints.

During 1986 there were a few comings and goings as the 1.3 CL was discontinued and replaced by the 1.6 CL – which was upgraded with internally adjustable mirrors, cloth trim, centre console, rear heater vents and velour carpets. Also, the base C model finally became available as a 5-door. However, 1987 meant more dramatic changes, starting in January when across the range a height-adjustable seat and top seat belt mounts were fitted along with

stereo radio/cassette systems. The GL gained the four-spoke steering wheel from the GTI, tinted glass, tweedy velour upholstery, padded gear knob and wider bedside strips. We could welcome back the Golf Driver this time with a 1,595cc, 75bhp, carburettor equipped engine. This 3-door was based on the CL, but distinguished by black wheel arch extensions and body sills, complemented by a centre console and Glencheck trim on the inside. Then in August the windscreen wipers were finally aligned for right hand drive cars. After years of peering beneath a dirty arc, drivers now benefited from a cleaner sweep of the screen as the wipers parked on the left. Not only that, the front quarterlights – which resulted in the door mirrors being positioned level with your ear – were eliminated. No wonder there was widespread jubilation throughout the land.

A four bar grille was fitted, with a silver Volkswagen roundel in the middle. At the back the rear badge was enlarged and centralized and the model script was italicized. Steering wheels were redesigned as were the column stalk controls, and the screen was sprayed clean with twin washer jets. The side rubbing strips and wheel arch surrounds were now fitted to the base model and the CL got bigger door bins. Finally the GL was fitted with electrically adjustable heated door mirrors and a central locking system covering the doors and fuel filler flap.

The big news in June 1988 was the return of the highly popular Driver, this time as a full production model. Now available as a 3-door and 5-door model it was distinguished by its GTI type accoutrements including twin halogen headlamps, 6J × 14in sports steel wheels and low profile tyres.

For August 1989 there were some minor specification changes as even the base

At last, wipers that parked on the left and door mirrors that sat sensibly at the end of window frame because the quarterlight was finally deleted. This is a facelifted 1987 model Golf. Pictured here is George Havell and one of those Golfs that go on for ever. Most remarkably the first 200,000 miles (320,000km) were covered with clutch crunching, kerb bumping learners in the driver's seat.

Mark 2 Golf CL (Catalyst)

Engine

	Four cylinder in line, toothed belt driven SOHC
	Alloy cylinder head, cast iron block transversely mounted in front
Capacity	1,595cc
Bore	81 × 77.4mm
Output	72bhp at 5200rpm
Compression ratio	9.0:1
Maximum torque	92lb/ft at 2700rpm
	Catalytic converter

Suspension

Front	Independent with MacPherson struts, lower wishbones, coil springs and anti-roll bar
Rear	Semi-independent with trailing arms, torsion beam, coil springs, telescopic dampers and anti-roll bar

Steering

Rack and pinion

Brakes

9.4in (239mm) ventilated front discs
Rear drums
Vacuum servo

Dimensions

Track – front	56.2in (1,427mm)
Track – rear	56in (1,422mm)
Wheelbase	97.4in (2,475mm)
Length	157in (3,988mm)
Width	66in (1,676mm)
Height	56in (1,422mm)
Ground clearance	4.5in (115mm)
Unladen weight	2,070lb (940kg)

Performance

Top speed	99mph (159kph)
Acceleration	0–60mph in 11.5 seconds

Fuel consumption

38.4mpg (7.3 litres per 100km)

The GTI look-alike Golf Driver, for posers who did not need the performance.

models were fitted with front door bins and the washer jets were now heated electrically. The CL got a four headlamp grille and the GL started to resemble the GTI even more closely as the front and rear bumpers were remoulded to incorporate spoilers bringing about the 'big bumper' look. Inside, a sports steering wheel was fitted and the velour went up another notch in quality. In the diesel department Volkswagen introduced a revised 1.6 turbo unit that featured a micro turbocharger and oxidation catalyst. It was badged as a GTD, a designation already used for some time on the Continent. Power increased to 80bhp making 0–62mph a relatively swift 13.2 seconds and top speed a comfortable 105mph (169kph).

GREEN GOLF

A year later Volkswagen launched the world's cleanest production car engine, the Umwelt. It was derived from the 1.6 naturally aspirated 54bhp unit, but a turbocharger and exhaust catalyser were added. Although the turbocharger increases power by 11 per cent its main function is to provide the engine with extra air for clean, smoke free running. In conjunction with the catalyst, more than half the aromatic hydrocarbons are eliminated – a lot less smelly than the average diesel.

Apart from the appearance of the Umwelt, 1990 was not that eventful. The Driver 5-door could now boast a steel sunroof, central locking and a split-fold rear seat. The CL was now catalysed and the power output dropped from 75 to 72bhp. Further up the range on the GL, power steering made parking easier and a sunroof let the sun shine in.

The following year, 1991, was the run-out year as the Mark 3 Golf was just months away from being announced – so the range was slimmed down and perked up to attract custom. There was the usual outbreak of special edition fever. At the bottom of the range, the Ryder was introduced in February. Based in the existing 1.3 base model it came with a sunroof, four head-lamp grille, split rear seat and velour upholstery. The 1.6 Driver got GTI wheel

A very clean looking engine bay, which belongs to an equally clean turbo diesel unit with an intercooler and badged as a GTD. Throughout the 1980s and 1990s Volkswagen continued to lead the way in oil burning engines, especially the Umwelt Diesel.

trims, white front indicator lenses, a tachometer, digital clock and improved upholstery. In October a Ryder version of the 1.6 came with wider Driver wheels, front head restraints, leatherette gear knob and gaiter, a light in the luggage compartment, plus a cover. A 1.8 Driver supplanted the GL. Meanwhile, the GTD Turbo got the Driver treatment and almost looked like the GTI.

The Mark 2 proved that the Golf could grow up physically and dynamically with-out losing its way. It may have lost some of its original charm, but the car had matured and now appealed to more car buyers than ever before. It confirmed beyond doubt that the leading 'Golf class' car still happened to be the Golf. For practicality, solidity and reliability it was hard to beat. But other manufacturers were doing their best to catch up and offer exciting alternatives. The Golf was still a class act, but for how long?

5   Too Hot to Handle?

'It has lost none of its magic' – *Motor*.

By 1984, every manufacturer in the world knew exactly what a GTI was. In particular they knew just how fast it should go, how it should handle and what it ought to look like. Whereas the old Golf GTI created and dominated the hot hatch sector, the new Golf had rivals ready and waiting to snatch the performance crown away. When it first arrived in the UK, *Motor* reviewed its performance and economy favourably. It addressed most of the old car's failings in terms of braking efficiency and accommodation. Only the Nissan Cherry Turbo could out-sprint the Golf as it reached 60mph in 8 seconds. However, the rivals were not only cheaper by £800 or more, but were also far better equipped.

In company with an MG Maestro and Volvo GLT, the Nissan was not a model to inspire the buying public. The closest rivals were undoubtedly the Ford Escort XR3i and Astra GTE. Neither was as refined or

A German specification Mark 2 GTI being put through its paces. The standard grille and small air dam, mark this out as a very early example.

65

well built as the Golf, and that explained the reason why someone would pay £1,000 more. *Motor* concluded that the GTI 'had lost none of its magic', although it was regarded as more of a sideways step than a dynamic leap forward.

The GTI was an integral part of the Mark 2 range announced in February

Mark 2 GTI

Engine

	Four cylinder in line, toothed belt driven SOHC
	Alloy cylinder head, cast iron block transversely mounted in front
Fuel injection	Bosch K-Jetronic
Capacity	1,781cc
Bore	81 × 86.4mm
Output	112bhp at 5800rpm
Compression ratio	10.0:1
Maximum torque	109lb/ft at 3500rpm

Transmission

	Front wheel drive
5-speed	3.46, 2.12, 1.44, 1.13, 0.89:1
Reverse	3.17:1
Final drive	3.67:1

Suspension

Front	Independent with MacPherson struts, lower wishbones, coil springs and anti-roll bar
Rear	Semi-independent with trailing arms, torsion beam, coil springs, telescopic dampers and anti-roll bar

The GTI gets 16 valves of fun. Apart from the subtle red badging and slightly lower ride height, there was little to tell the model apart.

Steering

Rack and pinion
3.7 turns lock to lock (power option 3.2)

Brakes

9.4in (239mm) ventilated front discs, 8.9in (226mm) solid rear discs
Vacuum servo

Tyres and wheels
Alloy   85/70HR-13 on 6J × 13
Steel   175/70HR-13 on 5.5 × 13

Dimensions
Track – front   56in (1,422mm)
Track – rear   56in (1,422mm)
Wheelbase   97in (2,464mm)
Length   157in (3,988mm)
Width   66in (1,676mm)
Height   55in (1,397mm)
Unladen weight (3-door) 2,026lb (920kg)
Unladen weight (5-door) 2,070lb (940kg)

Performance
Top speed   119mph (191kph)
Acceleration   0–60mph in 8.3 seconds

Fuel consumption
Urban   27.4mpg (10.3 litres per 100km)
Constant 56mph (90kph)   48.7mpg (5.8 litres per 100km)
Constant 75mph (121kph)   37.2mpg (7.6 litres per 100km)

Inside too, it was standard issue GTI, all the instruments and controls nicely grouped together in the line of sight, plus neat touches like the leather covered steering wheel, gear knob and gaiter. The 16-valve give-away is the red badge attached to the glove box.

1984. Modifications were as the standard cars, although there were disc brakes all round now and the 1.8 litre unit was a carry-over from the last incarnation of the GTI. This was effectively a Campaign specification GTI with lots of extras loaded on as standard – including Pirelli alloy wheels, steel sliding sunroof and metallic paint. On the outside the four lamp grille set it apart from lesser Golfs and there were red inserts on the bumpers. Despite being heavier, the new GTI had better aerodynamics, with the drag coefficient down from 0.42 to a more respectable 0.34, so speed and acceleration hardly suffered.

The first good news of 1985 came in February when the 5-door version was introduced to the UK market for the first time. Pirelli alloy wheels were standard although they had been deleted from the 3-door a few months earlier. By September of that year hydraulic tappets meant that adjustment was no longer part of the service schedule. Indicators were added to the

wings and at the front the spoiler became deeper.

AT LAST, SIXTEEN VALVES

September 1986 could simply have been the month when GTI got seat height adjusters and new style alloy wheels if it had not been for the dramatic arrival of the 3-door 16-valve. If you did not open the bonnet, the only clue that this had eight valves more than the standard GTI was a very subtle, bright red 16V badge below the existing logo. A closer look and a tape measure would also reveal that the car sat 0.4in (10mm) closer to the ground. Under the wheel arches there were also stiffer springs (10 per cent more at front, 20 per cent at the rear), modified shock absorbers and anti-roll bars. Even the ventilated front discs were larger at 10.4in (256mm), helped out by beefier brake pistons all round with ducts cut into the front spoiler

It is 1985 and 5-door practicality and performance in one GTI package finally land in the UK.

This is what the 16-valve unit looked like out of the confines of the engine department, sectioned so that we can get a closer look at its multi-valve workings.

to keep everything cool. At this range you might also spot that on the 6in rims were 185/60VR-14 tyres. Creature comforts included central locking, electric windows and a sunroof.

Under the bonnet was the 16-valve engine first seen powering the Scirocco. After the quick performance fix of bolting on turbos in the early 1980s, by far the more sophisticated and effective way of boosting power and increasing engine efficiency was to up the number of valves. Multi-valve cylinder heads was obviously the route to take so in November 1981 Volkswagen started development work.

The idea was to take the soon to be launched 1.8 and turn it into a higher torque unit that was more refined and could offer higher performance. Replacing the existing head with a cast-alloy thermally hardened 16-valve component was just part of the plan. In addition there were two counter-rotating camshafts connected by a chain, One moved pairs of 1.3in (32mm) diameter inlet valves while the other shifted the 1.1in (28mm) exhaust valves. These valves were competition specification, the inlet made from hardened steel and the outlet filled with sodium resulting in a 20 per cent improvement in gas flow. The valves were mated to hydraulic tappets that reduced mechanical noise and maintenance. To supply the extra oil required was the hard working oil pump from the diesel engine. A compression ratio of 10:1 and Bosch KA-Jetronic fuel injection system contributed a 24 per cent power increase on the 8-valve engine. This translated into 139bhp at 6,300rpm and a peak torque of 121.5lb/ft at 4,600rpm.

Mark 2 GTI 16-valve

Engine

Four cylinder in line, toothed belt driven SOHC
Alloy cylinder head, cast iron block transversely mounted in front
Bosch K-Jetronic fuel injection

Capacity	1,781cc
Bore	81 × 86.4mm
Output	139bhp at 6100rpm
Compression ratio	10.0:1
Maximum torque	133lb/ft at 4600rpm

The GTI gets even better in 1987 as the grille is simplified. Out go those annoying quarterlights, in come decent door mirrors, and the bumpers and side rubbing strips are beefed up.

Transmission

	Front wheel drive
5-speed	3.46, 2.12, 1.44, 1.13, 0.91:1
Reverse	3.17:1
Final drive	3.67:1

Suspension

	Lower ride height
Front	Independent with MacPherson struts, lower wishbones, uprated coil springs and anti-roll bar
Rear	Semi-independent with trailing arms, torsion beam, uprated coil springs (20 per cent stiffer), telescopic dampers and anti-roll bar

Steering

Rack and pinion
3.7 turns lock to lock (power option 3.2)

Brakes

Larger pistons, 10.1in (257mm) ventilated front discs, 8.9in (226mm) solid rear discs
Vacuum servo

Tyres and wheels

	185/60VR-13 on 6J × 14in alloys
1989	185/55VR-15 on 6J

Dimensions

Track–front	56in (1,422mm)
Track–rear	56in(1,422mm)
Wheelbase	97in (2,464mm)
Length	157in (3,988mm)
Width	66in (1,67mm)
Height	54.9in (1,395)
Unladen weight (3-door)	2,114lb (960kg)
Unladen wieght (5-door)	2,158lb (980kg)

Performance

Top speed	129mph (208kph)
Acceleration	0–60mph in 8.0 seconds

Fuel consumption

Urban	25.9mpg (10.9 litres per 100km)
Constant 56mph (90kph)	46.4mpg (6 litres per 100km)
Constant 75mph (121kph)	37.8mpg (7.4 litres per 100km)

HOT AND HIGH-TECH

The 1988 range upgrade in August 1987 brought the GTI a five slot grille and welcome relief from the quarterlights and the windscreen wipers that insisted on parking on the driver's side of the screen. Alloy wheels became optional on the 5-door. A digital instrument pack was added to the options list for the 16-valve, but there were few takers. 'Big bumper' models introduced in August 1989 were more aerodynamic and incorporated spoilers. The GTI logo was also moulded into the side rubbing strips. Front fog lamps were standard. The 16-valve benefited from a few extra trims, smoked rear light clusters and spoked alloy wheels, although electric windows were no longer standard.

Those 16-valve *aficionados* with families had to wait until January 1990 when the 5-door version was finally introduced. In October, though, the 16-valve got its electric windows back and the 8-valve became easy to park thanks to the addition of power steering as standard. The final 8-valve fling occurred a year later in October 1991 when it got the full 16-valve clone treatment, which amounted to BBS alloy wheels, electric front windows, smoked rear lenses, 16-valve style upholstery and standard metallic paint. By February 1992 the Mark 2 GTI story was all over.

SYNCHRONICITY

Volkswagen did not just build standard GTIs. With the Mark 2 in particular, they went the whole development hog with four wheel drive systems and superchargers. The Synchro hardly qualified as a hot Golf, but it did amount to a technically interesting car that glued itself to the road, could corner at a speed that would frighten a 16-valve and led directly to the brilliant Rallye. So let's take our hats off to the Golf Synchro, which made its debut at the 1985

Last of the GTI line. Here is a rear view of a 'big bumper' model.

Like a lot of interesting Golfs, only the badge gives this away as a permanent four wheel drive Synchro.

Frankfurt Motor Show and entered production five months after. It was available in CL trim and (depending on the intended market) was powered by either a 90bhp 1,781cc unit or a fuel injected catalyst version. Volkswagen made it look a little out of the ordinary and GTI-like with a large front spoiler, black wheel arch trims and sills, and inside there was a four-spoke steering wheel, padded dashboard and a centre console. But the big changes were underneath the otherwise unaltered Golf skin.

The four wheel drive system that Volkswagen chose was a sophisticated permanent one. It featured a viscous coupling made up of 59 steel plates contained within a round housing: 30 of the plates were fixed to the housing and the remaining 29 were fixed to a drive shaft connected to the rear differential. The power was transferred courtesy of a viscous silicon oil. The idea was to have slip-sensitive power distribution by integrating this viscous coupling into the drive train. This system would act like a centre differential, preventing wind ups in the drive train when there were differences in speed between front and rear wheels when negotiating corners. When something more dramatic happened, such as a wheel losing traction on ice, the plates connected more firmly

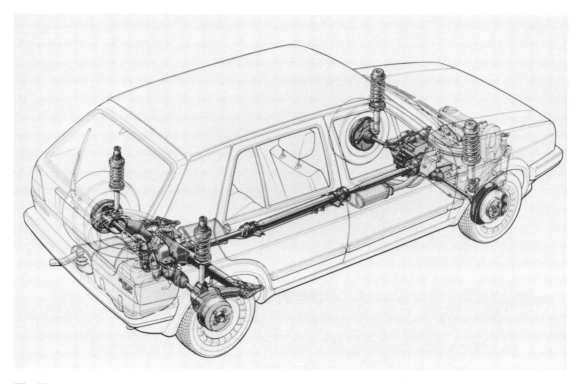

The X-ray vision view of the Synchro in all its four wheel drive, multi-differential glory.

and the optimum amount of torque was distributed from the front to the rear wheels. As a result the handling was more neutral while the maximum amount of usable power was employed by the system. In addition a freewheel was incorporated into the rear differential, which interrupted the flow of power to the axle under braking and allowed the four wheel drive system to work more effectively with the optional ABS system. What all this amounted to was a sophisticated four wheel drive system that no other manufacturer could match.

The Synchro upgrade did not stop at simply bolting on the four wheel drive system. For a start the floorpan had to be modified at the rear and the fuel tank reshaped accordingly. The penalty for this was a reduction in luggage space, down to 8.1cu ft (230 litres), but luckily a split rear seat was standard and boosted the available load space to 36.4cu ft (1030 litres). Underneath the floorpan the suspension was beefed up. At the back, semi-trailing arm axles were joined by MacPherson struts, stiffer springs and dampers plus an anti-roll bar. The width of the rear brake drum was also increased while up front the springs and dampers were also uprated.

Volkswagen followed up the original Synchro with a GT version in 1987. Most important, ABS brakes were standard, and the trim inside and out was raised to GTI levels. Although the weight went up by 220lb (100kg) compared with the standard front wheel drive model, performance of the Synchro was hardly affected.

COUNTRY LIFE

Not surprisingly, Volkswagen decided to take the four wheel drive concept to its logical conclusion and at the 1989 Geneva Motor Show exhibited the Montana. This was a proper offroad concept with decent ground clearance, sump protection and a radically raised bodywork courtesy of modified and spaced suspension. Power came from an injected 1.8 unit producing 98bhp. Renamed the Golf Country, it entered limited production in 1991.

The Golf Country.

RALLYE WINNER

Volkswagen's competition department had a secret weapon up their sleeves in 1989 and in expectation of the class of motor sport they expected to dominate, it was named Rallye. It had all the right World Rally Championship winning ingredients, including the Synchro four wheel drive system. The engine was not simply a warmed up GTI unit, but a revised 1.8 with a supercharger. Modifications amounted to a 80.6mm bore and 86.4mm stroke that reduced the displacement to 1,763cc. This move meant that the engine would qualify well within the prevailing 2.5 litre motor sport class requirements for supercharged

units at the time (which meant multiplying the capacity by 1.4).

With a compression ratio of 8:1 and a maximum supercharged boost pressure of 0.65 bar the engine produced 160bhp at 5,600rpm. All this was controlled by a Digifant electronic injection system. The G-Lader supercharger unit itself, so identified in Germany because of its housing shaped just like the seventh letter of the alphabet, was driven from the engine by a ribbed belt. Inside the unit were two interlocking snail shaped scrolls. A central oscillating lobe swept pockets of air along the spiral gallery towards the centre, from where the hot compressed air was channelled through the intercooler and into the

One of the most distinctive performance Golfs ever built, with unique rectangular headlights at the front and a bulging body kit. A 5,000 production run meant it was homologated for competition.

Rallye Golf G60

Engine

Four cylinder in line, toothed belt driven SOHC
Alloy cylinder head, cast iron block transversely mounted in front
Double belt driven G-Lader supercharger running at 1.6 times engine speed
Intercooler
Digifant fuel injection

Capacity	1,781cc
Bore	80.6 × 86.4mm
Output	60bhp at 5800rpm
Compression ratio	10.0:1
Maximum torque	166lb/ft at 3800rpm

Transmission

Synchro permanent wheel drive, viscous coupling
Modified Passat 5-speed gearbox

Suspension

	Ride height lowered by 0.4in (10mm)
Front	Independent with MacPherson struts, lower wishbones, coil springs and 0.9in (23mm) front anti-roll bar
Rear	Semi-independent with trailing arms, torsion beam, coil springs, uprated telescopic dampers and 0.8in (21mm) anti-roll bar

Steering

Rack and pinion
3.7 turns lock to lock (power option 3.2)

Brakes

9.4in (239mm) ventilated front discs, 8.9in (226mm) ventilated rear discs
Vacuum servo
Electronic ABS

Tyres and wheels

205/50R-15V on 6in rim alloys

Dimensions

Track – front	56.3in (1,430mm)
Track – rear	56.3in (1,430mm)
Wheelbase	97in (2,464mm)
Length	158.9in (4,035mm)
Width	66.9in (1,700mm)
Height	55.1in (1,400mm)
Unladen weight	2,632lb (1,195kg)

Performance

Top speed	130mph (209kph)
Acceleration	0–60mph in 7.6 seconds

Fuel consumption

Touring	28.5mpg (9.9 litres per 100km)

cylinders. This simple little unit boosted power from 112 to 160bhp.

Transmission duties were delegated to a new 5-speed gearbox first used in the Passat and destined to be fitted to the Corrado. The suspension was similar to the 16-valve except that the springs and shock absorbers had higher damping rates combined with stronger anti-roll bars. Keeping the Rallye in touch with the tarmac were 6J × 15in multi-spoke alloy wheels shod with 205/50VR-15 tyres. Volkswagen claimed that all this development work translated into a 0–62mph time of 8.6 seconds and top speed of 130mph (209kph). For all that effort, the Rallye was never used in anger on the rally circuit, even though they went to the trouble of building 5,000 left hand drive examples at the Volkswagen factory in Belgium. Still, it made a brilliant road car with a very good specification. It was hard to miss a Rallye with the front and rear bumpers remoulded to include aprons. Wheel arches were

Under the bonnet of the Rallye.

pumped outwards just like its big cousin the Audi Quattro Turbo. A special radiator grille and unique rectangular headlamps meant that there was no mistaking a Rallye in your rear view mirror. The lucky driver sat on half leather seats and could choose from a large range of extras.

SUPER G60

Although the Rallye was strictly a limited edition, it proved that there was a ready market eager to buy even hotter GTIs. So Volkswagen used the research and technology from the Rallye project to launch the G60. It joined the other G-Lader powered models – Passat Synchro, Corrado G60 and Polo G40 – at the top of the range.

Mechanically the car was slightly different from the Rallye, reverting to front wheel as opposed to four wheel drive. The engine was a 1,781cc GTI unit and with the G-Lader on board produced 160bhp at 5,800rpm. It was hitched up to a new MQ gearbox, which offered a set of low and closely spaced ratios. Top speed was in the region of 134mph (216kph) and 0–62mph was achieved in 8.3 seconds. Besides the usual subtle badging on the grille and off-side rear panel there were few distinguishing features to set this Golf apart. Unlike the Rallye it was available as a 5-door, but there were no wheel arch extensions or rectangular headlamps. On closer inspection, there were small differences – like the

Take your pick from either 5- or 3-door G60s. Available in left hand drive only with Rallye style alloy wheels or optional split rim BBS wheels, once again only the badge gives the performance game away.

Golf G60

Engine

Four cylinder in line, toothed belt driven SOHC
Alloy cylinder head, cast iron block transversely mounted in front
Double belt G-Lader supercharger running at 1.6 times engine speed
Intercooler
Digifant fuel injection

Capacity	1,781cc
Bore	81 × 86.4mm
Output	160bhp at 5800rpm
Compression ratio	10.0:1
Maximum torque	166lb/ft at 3800rpm

Transmission

Front wheel drive

5-speed	3.78, 2.12, 1.34, 0.97, 0.76:1
Reverse	3.68:1
Final drive	3.67:1

Suspension

Ride height lowered by 0.4in (10mm)

Front	Independent with MacPherson struts, lower wishbones, coil springs and 0.9in (23mm) front anti-roll bar
Rear	Semi-independent with trailing arms, torsion beam, coil springs, uprated telescopic dampers and 0.8in (21mm) anti-roll bar

Rack and pinion
3.7 turns to lock (power option 3.2)

Brakes

9.4in (239mm) ventilated front discs, 8.9in (226mm) ventilated rear discs
Vacuum servo
Electronic ABS

Tyres and Wheels

185/55R–15V on 6in rim alloys
195/50R–15V on 6.5in rim

Dimensions

Track–front	56.3in (1,430mm)
Track–rear	56.3in (1,430mm)
Wheelbase	97in (2,464mm)
Length	159.1in (4,040mm)
Width	66.9in (1,700mm)
Height	55.3in (1,405mm)
Unladen weight (3-door)	2,378lb (1,080kg)
Unladen weight (5-door)	2,434lb (1,105kg)

Performance
Top speed   134mph (216kph)
Acceleration   0–62mph in 8.3 seconds

Fuel consumption
Touring   28.5mpg (9.9 litres per 100km)

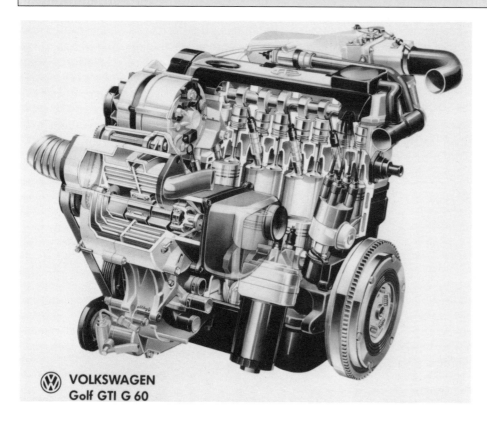

Inside the supercharged G60 engine, which pumped out an impressive 160bhp.

VOLKSWAGEN
Golf GTI G 60

0.2in (5mm) extra ride height – yet it was still a full 0.8in (20mm) lower at the front and 0.4in (10mm) at the rear compared to the standard 8-valve GTI. There were revised damper settings, Teflon coated suspension struts and thicker anti-roll bars. An option with 6.5in BBS cross-spoke alloy wheels and 195/50VR-15 tyres was also offered. Special equipment packs like the Edition One added Recaro seats, leather rim steering wheel and gear stick gaiter with chrome treated window surrounds on the tailgate and side windows.

NOT SO LIMITED

In 1990 Volkswagen came up with the Golf Limited. Under the bonnet was a supercharged 16-valve engine producing 210bhp coupled to the synchronized four wheel drive system; the 0–60mph time was a rapid 7.0 seconds.

There was very little on the outside to give the high performance game away. These models were all 5-door, finished in metallic black, with BBS cross-spoke alloy wheels and the twin headlamp grille from the lowliest L model. The occupants sat on leather and had electric windows to play with. The only thing limited about this model was the fact that just 70 were built.

GREATEST OF THEM ALL?

Enthusiasts will dispute the relative merits of the various GTIs and most will conclude that the original was the best in terms of purity and performance. But no one can deny that with the Mark 2 the GTI really came of age. It finally stopped on time and felt relaxed on a motorway without any compromises in handling. Not only that, the new generation Golf was developed as far as it could possibly go with superchargers, four wheel drive and 16 valves, making it one of the most exciting hatchbacks in the world. The variety and competence of the models offered has made it just as much a classic as the original version. This is more than can be said for the decidedly safe and sound Mark 3 – a GTI with all the character taken out. If the original Golf GTI was a lithe greyhound and the Mark 2 a strong, reliable and versatile Labrador cross, then the Mark 3 must be a poodle!

6 Safe and Sound – Golf Mark 3

'The metamorphosis of Golf 2 to 3 has been super conservative' – *Car.*

Seven years is a very long time in the motor industry. In that time new models come and go, technology takes a turn for the ever more complicated and tastes change. By the time that the Mark 3 Golf was launched, the automotive landscape had changed almost beyond recognition and all Volkswagen could do was keep up. While the original Golf was a beacon of innovation and the Mark 2 consolidated the success by winning many friends and influencing people, sadly the Mark 3 looked set to do no more than tread water.

The Mark 3 Golf takes shape from the drawing board.

Sectional dimension where the biggest, strongest and safest Golf is there for all to see.

ALSO RAN AND WINNER

In the Golf class, the Mark 3 is nothing exciting – a safe, solid and dependable buy. *Car* said as much when the car was launched and pointed out that models like the Peugeot 309, Fiat Tipo, Rover 200 and Citroen ZX had all injected welcome doses of fun, performance and refinement into the crowded hatchback market. People bought Golfs primarily because of the Volkswagen badge, which has always stood for toughness, reliability and quality. This is no bad thing really – buyers can be fickle when it comes to transient matters of style and almost indefinable qualities like fun. At the start or end of a long working day, most owners want a car that will start

first time and will not let them down. As a result the Golf has finally become a consumer durable rather than automotive icon. Nevertheless, it was voted European Car of the Year 1992.

The dashboard was a big improvement, with much more of a 1990s style. Its finish was fashionably smoother and, as ever, instruments and controls were grouped conveniently within sight and reach of the driver. Surrounding it all was a much more bloated body credited to Herbert Schéfer. When launched it really stood out from the crowd – it looked tall, and had oval headlamps that made it look blunt, yet it was no less aerodynamic than most of its rivals. Most critics were disappointed by the rear C-pillars, which had continued growing

Inside the slippery new Golf is an equally smooth approach to dashboard design.

since the Mark 1 and frankly made the car look almost like a van from certain angles. The trend at the time was to let more light in with a third panel of glass – as in the Ford Escort, Fiat Tipo and Citroen ZX – but Volkswagen insisted on a blind spot.

Bodily, the Mark 3 got bigger and safer. It was designed to pass tough American safety tests by being driven into a concrete wall at 33.5mph (54kph). (The Golf could survive an impact at 35mph or 56kph, so it exceeded the 1994 regulations.) To make it 30 per cent more rigid than the Mark 2 the sills and central door pillars were strengthened and the doors were reinforced. In addition, a rigid cross member ran behind the dashboard and another under the front seats. Seat belt tensioners, which tighten to the optimum position against the body in the event of a head-on collision, were installed in the front. Anti-submarining seats prevented the occupants from slipping underneath the lap belt in the event of a collision. Also the folding rear seat backrest had a sheet metal back to protect passengers from heavy objects in the load space being thrown forward. Finally, driver airbags were fitted as standard across the range from 1996.

The other preoccupation was environ-

European specification Golf G.

mental – Volkswagen believed that the manufacturers who produce the most cars have the greatest responsibility. That is why they opened a pilot plant for recycling in 1990 and were the first manufacturer to do so. The new Golf was fitted with about 60 per cent plastic parts that are completely recycled. The bumpers, battery, door pockets, water header and fuel tank can be recycled, and the inner wheel arch liners are manufactured out of recycled plastic. The Mark 3 Golf also cut down on noise pollution. Large volume silencers matched with carefully designed exhaust systems reduced outside noise substantially. Not only that, the environment inside the Golf is also quieter. That slippery new body – which looks bloated to some – is very aerodynamic, cutting down intrusive wind noise. The drag coefficient was reduced by 10 per cent compared with the Mark 2.

Depending on the model chosen it varied between 0.30 to 0.33. Larger wheel bearings reduced 'rolling' noise, and vibration was cut by the addition of new suspension and engine mountings. There was 22lb (10kg) more insulating material than on the Mark 2.

This was topped off with a new engine range that was slightly larger in capacity, but showed considerable improvements in efficiency, power and torque. Developments within the electronic engine management system helped. Compared to the previous model, drivers could save up to 10 per cent on fuel costs and produce cleaner emissions.

RANGE AND BADGING

The entry level engine fitted to the Golf L was a 60bhp, 1,390cc unit. For 1996, multi-

A 1996 specification Golf GL.

point fuel injection boosted economy up from 40.9 to 42.5mpg (6.6 to 6.9 litres per 100km) and the model was the best seller in five European countries. Revised specification on the L answered critics who felt that Volkswagens were 'basic'. Power steering, an electronic immobilizer, rear wash/wipe, split-folding rear seat and Sony radio/cassette were all standard. The mid range 1.6 also benefited from multi-point fuel injection.

There were two versions of the 1.8 engine. The lower output (75bhp) unit was used exclusively in the CL automatic. However, the remaining seven versions – CL, GL, Driver, 3-door, 5-door, manual and 4-speed automatic – were powered by the 90bhp engine. CL models had heat insulated tinted glass, driver's seat height adjuster, heated washer jets and central locking.

The Driver continued to be marketed as the 'insurance friendly' sports hatchback. It had Orlando 6J × 14in alloy wheels, locking wheel nuts and a rear spoiler. Customers could even specify red bumper inserts just like the original GTI. Inside, it was almost identical to a brand new GTI with the same cloth upholstery and the luxury of an electric sunroof. GL models exclusive to the 1.8, Umwelt and TDI range all had power windows, roofs and door mirrors.

GREEN DIESEL AND CLEAN RECHARGEABLE

The diesel 1.9 unit came in several states of tune, starting with a 64bhp model that for 1996 required less attention as the oil change intervals were extended from 5,000 miles (8,000km) to 10,000 miles

Golf Mark 3 1.8GL

Engine

Four cylinder in line, toothed belt driven SOHC
Alloy cylinder head, cast iron block transversely mounted in front
Monomotronic fuel injection
Catalytic converter

Capacity	1,781cc
Bore	81.0 × 86.4mm
Output	90bhp at 5500rpm
Compression ratio	10.0:1
Maximum torque	107lb/ft at 2500rpm

Transmission

Front wheel drive
5-speed

Suspension

Front	Coil springs and shock absorbers, suspension strut and lower wish bone, track stabilizing steering roll radius
Rear	Torsion beam axle, anti-roll bar

Steering

Power steering, rack and pinion

Brakes

Dual circuit, servo, asbestos free linings
Front discs, rear drums

Tyres and wheels

185/60R-14H on 6J × 14in alloys

Dimensions

Track – front	57.9in (1,470mm)
Track – rear	57.5in (1,460mm)
Wheelbase	97.4in (2,475mm)
Length	158.3in (4,020mm)
Width	66.5in (1,690mm)
Height	56.1in (1,425mm)
Unladen weight	2,387lb (1,084kg)

Performance

Top speed	107mph (172kph)
Acceleration	0–60mph in 12.7 seconds

Fuel consumption

32.2mpg (8.7 litres per 100km)

(16,000km). The good news did not end there as the average fuel consumption hit 49.8mpg (5.6 litres per 100km), which translates to a 500 mile (800km) range on a tank of diesel. If you had any rapeseed methyl ester handy, the engine would run on it without any modification. The Umwelt diesel continued to be successful, especially as the larger capacity and output (75bhp) provided the engine with extra air under load, reducing smoke. This model also featured a quick start pre-heating system to heat up the glow plugs when the driver's door was closed, so reducing the waiting time before starting.

Volkswagen's most economical diesel engine, the TDI, produced incredibly good consumption figures – 74.3mpg (3.8 litres per 100km) at a constant 56mph (90kph) or 900 miles (1450km) on a single tank. While most direct injection diesels are less powerful and noisier than indirect units, Volkswagen's direct system overcame these problems. Computer control of the fuel injection pump timing and the rate at which fuel is delivered into the combustion chamber from the injectors suppressed traditional diesel noise. The computer management system monitored the engine speed and corrected fuel delivery by changing fuel pump settings.

Switching off the engine every time you come to a halt sounded like a great way to save fuel, so Volkswagen decided to put it into practice. The Golf Ecomatic was the first production vehicle with an engine that would shut down automatically when it was not required. The clutch was operated

The driver of this TDI can afford to smile. According to Volkswagen's estimates he will make it to Paris without stopping for a refill.

by a vacuum servo unit controlled by electronics that stopped the engine when the accelerator was released and started it again when accelerating. (Overall, it is a unique driving experience. Stop in traffic and the engine switches off, engage first gear and it starts again. Take your foot off the accelerator when descending a hill and coast all the way down.) The standard 1.9 litre, 64bhp diesel engine provided the power and the resulting economy was an impressive 61mpg (4.6 litres per 100km) on the urban cycle.

For those who think that a diesel is an oil-guzzling environmental nightmare, there was an alternative. According to Volkswagen the extravagantly named Golf CitySTROMer was the world's first standard production car with electric propulsion. Introduced to the range in 1995, just 100 examples were offered for sale in Europe. The CitySTROMer drew its power from maintenance-free lead gel batteries that drove a synchronous motor with a continuous output of 18kW or 24bhp. This motor was connected to a conventional manual gearbox and clutch. Under the bonnet was a battery charger and voltage transformer that plugged into a standard socket. A single charge would take it 30 to

A Golf Ecomatic in action, or is that inaction? The engine switches itself off when stationary and starts as soon as the accelerator pedal is pressed.

The badge that proclaims to the world that this is a decidedly green Golf. The citySTROMer is powered by batteries.

37 miles (50 to 60km) in normal urban driving. Acceleration was lively for an electric car – 13 seconds to 31mph (50kph) – and it had a top speed of 62mph (100kph). Handling characteristics were kept Golf-like by positioning the batteries at front and rear for an even weight distribution, while power steering made parking easy.

Across the range, 5-speed manual gearboxes were standard, although the most exciting development happened to the automatic gearbox. An optional Electronic Programme Switch selected the sport programme if the accelerator was operated rapidly – full use was made of the engine power by delaying changing up to the next gear. Economy was selected when the accelerator was pressed slowly.

GOLFING ESTATE

Probably the most interesting extension to the Golf range has been the introduction of the estate in 1993, the first 'compact' model

---

Golf CitySTROMer

Power Plant

	3-phase synchronous motor, transversely mounted
Output	24bhp at 2250rpm
Maximum torque	75Nm at 3500rpm
Battery	44Ah

Transmission

	Front wheel drive, single-plate dry clutch
5-speed	3.45, 2.09, 1.47, 1.10, 0.81:1
Reverse	3.38:1
Final drive	4.26:1

Suspension

Front	Coil springs and shock absorbers, suspension strut and lower wishbone, track stabilizing steering roll radius
Rear	Torsion beam axle, anti-roll bar

Steering

Power steering, rack and pinion

Brakes

Dual circuit, servo, asbestos free linings
Discs

Tyres and wheels

175/70R-13T on 5.5J × 13

Dimensions

Track–front	58.2in (1,478mm)
Track–rear	56.8in (1,442mm)
Wheelbase	97.4in (2,475mm)
Length	158.3in (4,020mm)
Width	66.7in (1,695mm)
Height	55.3in (1,405mm)
Unladen weight	3,500lb (1,589kg)

Performance

Top speed	62mph (100kph)
Acceleration	0–31 in 13 seconds

Range per charge

Urban driving	31 to 37 miles (50 to 60km)
Constant 50mph (80kph)	37 to 50 miles (60 to 80km)
Constant 31mph (50kph)	44 to 56 miles (70 to 90km)

to be built at Wolfsburg. Officially Volkswagen reckoned they could trace the concept all the way back to the Type 3 Variant, which, in their words, 'initiated the Volkswagen estate philosophy: building versatile and extremely spacious cars primarily designed for private use'. The company was responding to an increasing demand for a growing market segment, as one buyer in seven wants an estate. It is strange that the hatchback concept, popularized by the original Golf, had not killed off the estate or the saloon. An estate body is the most logical utilization of space, but logic has little to do with buying habits or car building trends. Increasingly, customers want a vehicle that looks purposeful. As the car is increasingly under attack

the best defence is to justify one on the grounds that it is, or may be useful – hence Volvos. But estates can have style (witness the cramped BMW Touring) and class (like the expensive T series Mercedes). So what Volkswagen have done is to make a compact, stylish and above all practical estate car.

The four door estate was 13in (320mm) longer than the Golf with 16.5cu ft (466 litres) of luggage space, which amounted to 40 per cent more than the standard hatchback. Folding the asymmetric split seat forwards gave a flat surface 66.9in (1,640mm) long and a maximum volume of 50.3cu ft (1425 litres). If you wanted to play three seaters there was 39.9cu ft (1130 litres) of space and as a four seater you were down

For those with a ready made lifestyle the Golf Estate can accommodate most bulky hobbies.
Pictured is a European GT and the load bay of a UK specification estate.

to 30.5cu ft (865 litres). The roof rails offered even more load space.

The main technical difference between the hatchback and estate was the revised rear axle. It allowed the luggage space to be as flat as possible. In addition the suspension struts were inverted to reduce the amount of room taken up by the turrets, leaving 39.4in (1,000mm) of clear loading width between the rear wheel arches. Rubber rear axle mountings taken from the Passat meant that the estate could cope with much higher loads than the hatchback. These mountings also steered passively, reducing any deviations in the track when cornering sharply. The combination of a longer tail and space-saving rear axle also meant that there was room for a 13.2 gallon (60 litre) fuel tank and with the TDI model that resulted in a whopping range of 685 miles (1100km).

The all important tailgate ran down to the bumper, and lifted up on pneumatic struts to make life easier.

GOLF STONED

The 'Rolling Stones Collection' came about because Volkswagen sponsored their 1995 European and South American 'Voodoo Lounge' tours. In the group's home country buyers could choose between a 1.6 model and a very limited edition (around 25) 1.8 Cabriolet. The package consisted of special upholstery, and graphics from the Voodoo Lounge album were used on the inside and outside. Volkswagen tried hard to justify the connection with the Rolling Stones: 'The Stones fans and our potential customers are the same people. Driving and music have gone together since radios were

A Rolling Stones special edition Golf with 'Voodoo Lounge' graphics.

first put into cars. The band was on the road with us as far back as 1963, they made their first tour of Britain in a Volkswagen bus – the legendary Bully.'

GOLF BELOW PAR?

By the time *Car* got around to comparing the new Golf with its rivals, they pronounced the model 'below par'. A 1.8 CL was pitched against a Citroen ZX Aura, Ford Escort 1.8 LX and Mitsubishi Colt 1.6 GLXi and found wanting. Although quiet at speed, it had trouble exceeding 100mph (161kph) and was regarded as mundane transport. Handling was exemplary as ever, and the steering easily the best of the group. Driving position was just about perfect too, with superb seats. When it came to

driver appeal, they reckoned it was almost impossible to extract any pleasure at all from driving the new Golf. What *Car* and a lot of other magazines and buyers spotted was a drop in build quality – the fit and finish were just not up to the old Volkswagen standards.

At the best of times, a Golf that is not a GTI is hard to get in a lather about. The Mark 3 in particular has switched categories over three generations from revolutionary to reliable and ultimately dull. More than ever the Mark 3 is little more than a domestic appliance with a very long extension lead. Although it might be inoffensive and forgettable, scratch the surface and you will find traces of the original model underneath. After all, the suspension is pure Mark 1 and the engines can be traced right back to the earliest Audi 80.

Golf2

VW

Golf3

GOLF 2 (1984-91) BIGGER, STRONGER BODY 7" LONGER AND 2" WIDER THAN GOLF 1. A WIDE RANGE OF PETROL AND DIESEL ENGINES. 1988 SYNCRO FOUR WHEEL DRIVE MODEL.

GOLF 3 (1991-?) BIGGER, SAFER AND BLOBBIER MODEL WITH USUAL RANGE OF PETROL AND DIESEL UNITS, PLUS 8V GTI 16V IN 1993 AND RANGE TOPPING VR6

JETTA 2 (1984-92) 12" EXTRA LENGTH MEANT 23 CU.FT OF LOAD SPACE AND A VERY BIG BOOT. ALSO SEVERAL 'INTERESTING' MODELS, 8V AND 16V GTIs, ALSO SYNCRO

VENTO (1992-?) BOOTED GOLF NOW RENAMED, BUT SIMILAR RANGE OF MODELS TO HATCHES WITH PETROL, DIESEL AND TURBO DIESELS INCLUDING VR6.

GOLF GTI (1984-91) 8V MODEL AND FROM 1985 16V, JOINED BY A BRACE OF PERFORMANCE GOLFS. 1990 SUPERCHARGED G60 1989 FOUR WHEEL DRIVE RALLYE AND 210BHP LIMITED

ESTATE (1993-?) A NEW GOLF BODYSTYLE WHICH IS 32 CM LONGER THAN THE HATCHBACK WITH 466 LITRES OF LUGGAGE SPACE.

CORRADO (1989-95) GOOD LOOKING COUPE' BASED ON GOLF 2 WITH KARMANN BODY AND EXCITING 16V, SUPERCHARGED G60 AND IN 1992 VR6 ENGINES.

CABRIOLET (1993-?) KARMANN BUILD AN ALL NEW OPEN TOP ON GOLF 3 PLATFORM WITH 1.8, 2.0 & DIESEL UNITS.

© 1996 JAMES RUPPERT

96

Larger rear lights clusters on the Mark 1 Golf from 1982.

In July 1981 the Golf fascia and interior were restyled, with the instruments being regrouped behind a non-reflective panel, better ventilation and repositioned door pulls. The GTI pictured here benefited from padded four-spoke steering wheel and striped seats.

1.8 litre power for the Mark 1 GTI from September 1982. A bored out 1.6, the pistons were lightened and crankshaft revised. This raised output to 112bhp and 0–60 went down to just over 8 seconds.

Arguably the finest GTI of all: the limited edition
Campaign was the Mark 1's swansong and came with
Pirelli alloy wheels, tinted glass, metallic paint, sunroof
and leather covered steering wheel as standard.

The distinctive four headlamp grille introduced with the
Campaign and a feature of Mark 2 model as well.

This is the final Mark 2 GTI incarnation, the so-called
'big bumper' version launched in August 1989 which
featured smooth bumpers with integral spoilers and the
GTI logo moulded into the side rubbing strips.

It's the revised rear end of the Golf 2, but still with Giugiaro's trademark wraparound tailgate.

GTI's Mark 1 and 2 together. The later car may be bigger and heavier, but it is more aerodynamic so performance hardly suffered.

Inside a Mark 3 Golf, the fascia is smoother and even more ergonomically friendly. Note the non-standard Momo Monte Carlo steering wheel.

Smoother styling on the outside for the Mark 3. It retains the thick C pillars, but the owner has replaced the plain GTI Le Mans alloys with spoked ones by Speedline.

The Mark 3 has a much deeper tailgate, but there is a close family resemblance to the previous model.

Mark 3 Golf: bigger, safer, but softer and slower. This GTI has been subtly modified for the better with lowered suspension, deeper Bonarth splitter spoiler and Kamei 'eyebrows'.

The GTI engine increased in size to 2.0 litres in 1991. Output though was the same as the old pre-catalyst 1.8. Colin Stone, owner of this car, has boosted output to 133bhp. Noted K & N air filter and Eibach strut brace.

Volkswagen insisted on adequate luggage space when Karmann opened up the Golf. As a result the hood sits on the rear deck.

Rivage was the run out model for the last two years of the cabriolet's life and featured Le Castellet alloy wheels.

The Karmann Cabriolet lasted for 13 years, spanning three generations of Golf. This Rivage has heated front seats, tinted glass and electrically operated hood.

Practical and reliable: the highly popular Caddy built in Yugoslavia from 1982. This one works for a living even though smartened up with cross spoke alloys and colour keyed paint work.

Caddy's tailgate makes loading the pick-up easier.

From the rear it is easy to see how the Rallye differs from the standard Golf, with its side skirts, blistered wheel arches and colour keyed bumpers.

Golf Rallye, the most magnificent Golf of all. Behind those distinctive, rectangular headlamps is a supercharged engine and keeping it all on the road is a Synchro four-wheel drive system.

Left-hand drive only for the motorsport homologated Golf Rallye. Seats are half leather.

The Golf could have looked like this. Three interpretations from the Italdesign studio in the early 1970s.

A full size styling model for the US market Rabbit showing how the three and five door versions would look. The rectanglar headlamps proposed for the original European Golf would make it to the finished US specification model.

7   Hot Mark 3

'The new Golf showed Grandad how it should be done' – Roger Bell, *Car.*

Car were the first to road test the new GTI in the UK and went about the task in the best manner possible, by bringing together the three GTI generations. A pristine 14,000 mile (22,500km) 1979 Mark 1, a last-of-line 1991 1.8 and a brand new 2.0 litre vied for comparison and Roger Bell found the difference between the original and latest incarnation 'cosmic'. Luckily, the Mark 2 was on hand as the link between the two eras from the practical and

Evolution, or downward spiral? All three GTI generations together – which would you choose?

unpretentious original to the civilized family hatchback that is the Mark 3 Golf GTI.

The new GTI had a larger 2.0 litre engine with a Digifant multi-point electronic fuel injection and ignition system and a regulated catalytic converter. Engine size increased to 1,984cc by enlarging the bore and stroke to 82.5mm and 92.8mm respectively. Power output rose to 115bhp at 5,400rpm. Torque, at 122lb/ft, was up 7 per cent and was produced at 3,200rpm. Officially, maximum speed was 123mph (198kph), while 0–62mph took 10.1 seconds. On the outside the GTI was distinguished by its colour-coded two bar grille, black wheel arches and bumper extensions. The rear light clusters had darkened lenses and a spoiler framing the top of the rear

window. In addition, 6.5J × 15in Long Beach alloy wheels, twin exhaust pipes and twin headlights were fitted. Inside there were sports seats, electric windows, an on-board computer and a height-adjustable sports steering wheel.

OLD, NEW AND NEARLY NEW

It was immediately apparent during *Car*'s assessment that the Golf had been putting on weight over the years. The original Golf weighed in at 1,860lb (844kg) and with the Mark 3 it was up to 2,274lb (1,032kg). That was hardly surprising in the light of the extra room, equipment and sophistication involved. Not surprisingly the new car has

Mark 3 GTI at home on the Autobahn.

a poorer power to weight ratio of 113bhp per ton as against 133, but a better torque to weight ratio, with 120lb/ft per ton against 122. The extra gears and more aerodynamic body helped it to a much higher top speed – 120mph (193kph) compared to 108mph (174kph) – and a marginally better 0–60mph time of 8.7 seconds against 9.6 seconds. Maybe a much better comparison would be with the last incarnation of the original GTI with a 1.8 engine and 5-speed gearbox, which would embarrass a Mark 3 – and a Mark 2 for that matter – in performance. Weight (135bhp per ton) and torque (131lb/ft per ton) ratios of the 1.8 GTI resulted in a 0–60mph time of 8.0 seconds, which has never been bettered by an 8-valve GTI. It is worth remembering, though, that the old Mark 2 was strangled by a catalyser in its last years that increased weight and reduced output from 112 to 108bhp. That alone made the new 2.0 litre GTI worth waiting for, with its larger engine.

Best of all, the car turned out to be quieter and much more refined than its predecessors. The major contributory factors to this more relaxed state of affairs was the revised chassis and aerodynamics. Underneath it all was a Mark 2 set-up, but the ride was more supple and less harsh. Power steering might have deadened the responses, but it is nonetheless very sharp and more relaxing to drive – fast or slow. And there is no doubt that coming to a halt in a 2.0 litre with its standard ABS brakes is much safer than the unreliable disc and drum configuration of the original model.

Dynamics and mechanics aside, the interior of the new car was a smoothly sculpted delight. The sports seats held on firmly yet comfortably to the front passengers and

The new GTI from the rear three quarters, classy and subtle as usual.

the instruments were clustered together for the driver. The finish was improved and the ventilation better. The original Golf had tiny vents and the Mark 2 had curious knuckle high, mid mounted openings, but now the dashboard sat higher and provided plenty of fresh air. But there was one major omission: no golf ball topped gear stick! The most offensive thing about it was that ever-expanding blind spot otherwise known as the C pillar.

Nothing stays the same and you cannot really compare models separated by thirteen years. Cars get better and all Volkswagen have done is grow up with their customers, who demand more comfort and refinement. Volkswagen would have been criticized if they produced a raw street racer and Roger Bell reckoned that the supercharged Polo G60 was the spiritual successor to the original GTI. If progress is to be measured in terms of safety and refinement then the 2.0 litre Mark 3 GTI has to be the best Golf yet, even though it is not the best GTI.

NEW GOLF GTI TAKES ON THE REST

The Mark 3 should have been better than its ancestors but it could not afford to fall behind its direct competitors. A month after pitching the 2.0 litre GTI against the old timers, *Car* trotted out the Fiat Tipo 16V, Nissan Sunny GTI and Ford Escort XR3i. Immediately the GTI, constantly criticized for putting on weight, shaped up as the lightest of all at 2,282lb (1,037kg). Where it seemed to lose out though was in the engine, as all the other cars had 16 valves and significantly better power to weight ratios. This translated into the Golf bringing up the rear in all the performance tests; *Car* described it as 'genteel'.

However, the car redeemed itself when it came to handling. Of all the cars it was judged to be the safest and most rewarding to drive. The 'Plus' suspension system used by Volkswagen could not be described as sporting in the traditional sense, yet it suppressed torque steer and aided stability so that steering, grip and body control was faultless. It featured a revised front axle so that the distance between the steering axis and the point of wheel contact with the road surface shrunk from 2.1in (52mm) to 1.6in (40mm). At the back matched spring/damper rates, with gas filled dampers, ensured good road adhesion at all times. Overall the suspension lowered the ride height by 0.4in (10mm) at the front and 0.8in (20mm) at the rear. The power assisted steering was also much firmer. Equally impressive were the fascia and comfortable driving position. However, the test's conclusion had some good and bad news. Plus points were the traditional GTI qualities of poise and build integrity. Against that was the fact that the car had fallen way behind in terms of performance; the low equipment levels and high price made it even more uncompetitive. The Tipo came out top, although it has never proved to be a big seller or ultimately all that durable.

EIGHT VALVES GOOD, SIXTEEN VALVES BETTER?

Two years after the new GTI failed to impress, Volkswagen sought to put things right by introducing a 16-valve version. Where the eight had been sluggish, less sporting and a bit soggy, the sixteen had to redress the balance. As *Car* unkindly observed on the cover of their December 1992 issue: 'Golf loses its balls'.

The 8-valve Golf had proved that the nature of the GTI had changed radically.

GTI 8-valve

Engine

Four cylinder in line, toothed belt driven SOHC
Alloy cylinder head, cast iron block transversely mounted in front
Digifant fuel injection
Catalytic converter
Lambda control

Capacity	1,984cc
Bore	82.5 × 92.8mm
Output	115bhp at 5400rpm
Compression ratio	10.4:1
Maximum torque	166Nm at 3200rpm

Transmission

Front wheel drive

5-speed	3.45, 1.94, 1.29, 0.97, 0.81:1
Reverse	3.17:1
Final drive	3.67:1

Suspension

Front	Coil springs and shock absorbers, suspension strut and lower wishbone, track stabilizing steering roll radius
Rear	Torsion beam axle, anti-roll bar

Steering

Power steering , rack and pinion

Brakes

Dual circuit, servo asbestos free linings
Ventilated front discs, solid rear

Tyres and wheels

185/60VR-14T on 6.5J × 15in alloys

Dimensions

Track – front	57.1in (1,450mm)
Track – rear	56.5in (1,434mm)
Wheelbase	97.4in (2,475mm)
Length	158.3in (4,020mm)
Width	66.7in (1,695mm)
Height	55.3in (1,405mm)
Unladen weight (3-door)	2,610lb (1,185kg)
Unladen weight (5-door)	2,676lb (1,215kg)

Performance

Top speed	124mph (200kph)
Acceleration	0-60mph in 10.1 seconds

Fuel consumption

35.4mpg (7.9 litres per 100km)

Gone were the hyperactive hot hatchbacks of old and in came refined, road-eating family hatchbacks – they got safe and boring. So if you wanted a truly exciting Golf, the 16-valve should have been worth waiting for. This time the 16-valve head had the new 2.0 litre unit underneath it that produced 150bhp at 6000rpm instead of 115bhp and was quite distinct from the units fitted to the Corrado and the Passat. New valves and revised breathing were designed to provide extra power and low down torque. The result was a much happier 0–60mph in a useful 8 seconds and a top speed of 134mph (216kph). The 5-speed gearbox was carried over from the 8-valve GTI, as was the suspension. Once again the handling was reckoned to be safe and predictable, yet still fun.

There was a traction control system that eliminated torque steer by working in conjunction with the ABS braking system. It monitored the speed of the driving wheels up to 25mph (40kph), so that when a difference in the driving wheel was detected, the system would brake the spinning wheel. *Car* pitched it in with the Citroen ZX 16V and Honda Civic VTi. It lost out mainly on price to the better equipped Citroen although it was fun to drive, while the flawed Civic rewarded the enthusiast and was good value. What the test proved was that the GTI was no longer the driver's favourite.

A GTI OR NOT A GTI

Whatever you do, do not call the VR6 a GTI, because it is not, it is much better – that was Volkswagen's approach at the time and it is difficult to disagree. The VR6 was something for GTI owners to aspire to. Not overtly sporting, but no slouch either, it combined comfort with performance clout. It was more of a scaled down silky engined Mercedes or Audi. So there you have it: a luxury car in a handy hatchback package.

If you lived in America you had to call the VR6 a GTI, because that is the only Mark 3 performance Golf they got. It was most definitely not a GTI, just Volkswagen's boldest and most welcome move to date – installing the superb V6 engine first seen in the Corrado and Passat. (The Golf VR6 got the Passat 2.8 174bhp version, rather than the Corrado 190bhp 2.9.) The narrow 15-degree engine sat snugly and transversely between the front wheels. The 5-speed gearbox from the GTI was modified and strengthened to cope with VR6 power. Wheelspin was kept to the minimum by a traction control system that works at speeds below 25mph (40kph).

VR6 BEATS BMW

Before it was launched in February 1992

COLOUR CONCEPT

Available for the 1996 model year, the Volkswagen Golf GTI Colour Concept was the most flamboyant GTI ever launched. A splash of colour was the overriding theme. Outside, the Colour Concept was available in a choice of vibrant yellow, red, blue, or green. Leather in the same colour as the exterior covered the standard heated Recaro seats, doors, gear knob and gaiter. The steering wheel was also leather rimmed, with colour matched stitching. Other unique features of the Colour Concept were 6.5J × 15in six-spoke Solitude alloy wheels and silver faced instruments. For those who did not fancy being the centre of attention there was a subtle all black edition too.

GTI 16-valve
Engine

Four cylinder in line, toothed belt driven DOHC
Alloy cylinder head, cast iron block transversely mounted in front
Digifant fuel injection, catalytic converter, Lambda control

Capacity	1,984cc
Bore	82.5 × 92.8mm
Output	150bhp at 6000rpm
Compression ratio	10.4:1
Maximum torque	180Nm at 4800rpm

Transmission

Front wheel drive

5-speed	3.30, 1.94, 1.31, 1.03, 1.84:1
Reverse	3.06:1
Final drive	3.68:1

Suspension

Front	Coil springs and shock absorbers, suspension strut and lower wishbone, track stabilizing steering roll radius
Rear	Torsion beam axle, anti-roll bar

Steering

Power steering, rack and pinion

Brakes

Dual circuit servo, asbestos free linings
Ventilated front discs, solid rear

Tyres and wheels

205/50VR-15V on 6.5J × 15in alloys

Dimensions

Track – front	57.1in (1,450mm)
Track – rear	56.5in (1,434mm)
Wheelbase	97.4in (2,475mm)
Length	158.3in (4,020mm)
Width	66.7in (1,695mm)
Height	55.3in (1,405mm)
Unladen weight (3-door)	2,731lb (1,240kg)
Unladen wegiht (5-door)	2,797lb (1,270kg)

Performance

Top speed	134mph (216kph)
Acceleration	0–60mph in 8.7 seconds

Fuel consumption

33.2mpg (8.5 litres per 100km)

Golf VR6, two more cylinders than any other model and a very impressive 174bhp mean superhatch 140mph (225kph) performance. Not only that, this German registered example also has a four wheel drive synchro undercarriage. Brilliant.

onto the UK market *Car* logically pitched the VR6 against its closest rival, the straight six cylinder BMW 325i. Producing 192bhp, with 177lb ft of torque, the BMW lost these advantages when its weighty 2,856lb (1,296kg) was taken into a account against the Volkswagen's 2,542lb (1,154kg). The result was a better power to weight ratio for the VR6 at 153bhp/ton, by 3bhp. In terms of performance the VR6 won, getting to 60mph in 6.9 seconds (7.6 seconds for the 325i) and reaching a top speed of 138mph (222kph), just a shade faster than the BMW. The Bavarian car did score well when it came to putting its power into practice, being positive and stable, while the VR6 could scrabble about quite alarmingly when pushed. Nevertheless the Volkswagen was judged to have taken the GTI concept several steps further, deep into the heartland of

sporty luxury usually occupied by BMW. It was quicker and more comfortable and a worthy superior to the GTI.

The specification was of course high, and exceeded the 16-valve's equipment list by having a passenger air bag, front fog lights, leather steering wheel, rear head rests, electric glass tilt/slide sunroof and Isola cloth upholstery. For the 1996 model year the VR6 got an even more up market and subtle look. It lost the black bumper tops and wheel arch extensions, which were replaced by a completely colour coded body.

What must be regarded as the flagship model for the whole Golf range was the Highline – the ultimate VR6. Buyers could choose between two colours, Diamond Black Pearl, or Purple Violet Pearl with matching leather interior. The manual gearbox version had a walnut topped gear lever, and all versions came with variable

Golf VR6

Engine

15-degree V6 cylinder SOHC
Alloy cylinder head, cast iron block transversely mounted in front
Bosch Motronic fuel injection

Capacity	2,792cc
Bore	81 × 90.3mm
Output	174bhp at 5000rpm
Compression ratio	10.0:1
Maximum torque	235Nm at 4200rpm

Transmission

Front wheel drive

5-speed	3.30, 1.94, 1.31, 1.03, 0.84:1
Reverse	3.06:1
Final drive	3.68:1

Suspension

Front	Coil springs and shock absorbers, suspension strut and lower wishbone, track stabilizing steering roll radius
Rear	Torsion beam axle, anti-roll bar

Steering

Power steering, rack and pinion

Brakes

Dual circuit servo, asbestos free linings
Ventilated front discs, solid rear

Tyres and wheels

205/50VR-15V on 6.5J × 15in alloys

Dimensions

Track – front	57.1in (1,450mm)
Track – rear	56.5in (1,434mm)
Wheelbase	97.4in (2,475mm)
Length	158.3in (4,020mm)
Width	66.7in (1,695mm)
Height	55.3in (1,405mm)
Unladen weight (3-door)	2,830lb (1,285kg)
Unladen weight (5-door)	2,896lb (1,315kg)

Performance

Top speed	141mph (227kph)
Acceleration	0–60mph in 7.6 seconds

Fuel consumption

28.9mpg (9.7 litres per 100km)

heating front seats and manual air conditioning. Not surprisingly the options list was empty – according to Volkswagen 'it has got it all'.

The latest GTI incarnation was very different from those that went before. However, the VR6 was so much more than the performance Golfs of earlier years. Surely there has been a Golf to suit everyone's taste?

This is the UK market specification VR6 Highline, the most luxurious Golf of them all.

Inside the VR6 Highline, there is hide as far as the bottom can wriggle and hands can reach.

THE SPIRIT LIVES ON

Perhaps the spirit of the original GTI lives on in another model, in another part of the Volkswagen Group. The Seat Ibiza GTi has stylish and chunky bodywork designed by – guess who? – Giugiaro. Underneath the bonnet beats the 2.0 litre engine that also powers the Golf GTI. The Seat is much lighter – 2,026lb (920kg) compared to 2,246lb (1,020kg) – which means a more responsive and exciting package. It is cheaper than the Golf and there is even a 16-valve version that is even more potent. If you want the old fashioned GTI experience, the answer is simple: buy a Seat Ibiza GTi.

The Seat Ibiza GTi, spiritually the GTI's successor. The author drove this one for nine months and adored every moment.

Hot Golfs

SPORT GOLF (1973-74) PROTOTYPE GOLF WITH AUDI 80 ENGINE & FUEL INJECTION = GTI

GTI (1975-82) ORIGINAL 1·6 INVENTED THE 'HOT HATCH' AND THE REST WAS HISTORY.

GTI CONVERTIBLE (1980-93) GLI & GTI VERSIONS EARLY ON AS KARMANN AND VW COMBINED CABRIOLET AND HOT HATCH CONCEPTS

GTI 1·8 (1982-83) BIGGER 1·8 ENGINE WHICH BOOSTED OUTPUT TO 112 BHP. MODEL RUN OUT 'CAMPAIGN' WITH ALLOYS AND SUNROOF.

G60 (1990-91) SUPERCHARGED GTI WITH REVISED SUSPENSION, ABS BRAKES AND 160 BHP. 3 AND 5 DOOR OPTIONS

GOLF 2 GTI (1984-91) LONGER AND WIDER IN HOUSE (VW) STYLED BODYWORK WITH 1·8 ENGINE. 16V MODEL FROM 1985

GOLF LIMITED (1990) ONLY 70 BUILT WITH FOUR WHEEL DRIVE AND 210 BHP SUPERCHARGED ENGINE & 142 MPH.

RALLYE (1989) 5,000 BUILT FOR RACING HOMOLOGATION WITH G60 SUPERCHARGED ENGINE, FOUR WHEELDRIVE & BODYKIT

GOLF VR6 (1991-?) NARROW ANGLE V6 2·8 UNIT PRODUCING 174 BHP. AUTOMATIC TRANSMISSION 1993, BADGED AS GTI IN USA.

GOLF 3 GTI (1991-) SOFTER, SAFER & SLOWER BUT WITH LARGER 2·0 ENGINE 1993 16V WITH 150 BHP RESTORES PERFORMANCE

© 1996 JAMES RUPPERT

8 Drag Acts – Scirocco and Corrado

'The ideal enthusiast's car: the racer you drive to the grocery store' – *Road Test* magazine.

Giugiaro had a problem with the Golf. It was too small, and he believed that Volkswagen were out of date if they were expecting to compete with larger models like the Fiat 128. The problem was that the dimensions were budgeted and immovable. Giugiaro turned these restrictions into a positive advantage with a revolutionary shape that evolved into the Golf. Even so, he pointed out that such a short wheelbase would make the perfect basis for a 2+2 coupé. Volkswagen, however, were not remotely interested.

SEARCHING FOR COUPÉS

Just as the success of the Beetle had stifled

You cannot have one without the other. In the beginning designer Giugiaro had the dimensions that defined the new Golf. He proposed a coupé, which was rejected, but his and Karmann's persistence paid off. As a result, the Scirocco was launched before the Golf.

its replacement, the Karmann Ghia coupé outstayed its welcome by the 1960s and was overdue for replacement. Indeed, Ghia were constantly sending Karmann suggestions for updating the tired old coupé –

from simple scale drawing facelifts to full size models of proposed replacement bodies. The last Ghia proposal made by Karmann was designed by Giugiaro in 1967 and called the Type 1 convertible. The

This is the model that had to be replaced, the Karmann Ghia.

This Type 1 Cabriolet proposal in 1965 was styled by Giugiaro, but was never produced.

This Volkswagen 914 was never intended as a Karmann Ghia replacement, yet it never succeeded as a prestigious coupé either, even with a Porsche badge.

Italian designer would inevitably crop up again, but in the meantime Karmann Ghia had more luck finding outlets for new coupés in far flung Brazil. Having set up a branch there they went on to build 23,577 between 1970 and 1973. Like the old European model it was based on the Type 1 chassis, but at least it had more contemporary styling.

Back home, Karmann began assembling

These coupés (1970–73 and 1973–76) styled by Karmann were big in Brazil, but never made it to America or Europe.

the Porsche 914/4 in 1969, a mid flat four engined, air cooled Targa, which looked like a replacement for the old Karmann Ghia. However, this radically different model did not fit comfortably into the Volkswagen model line-up and was in a different price bracket anyway. Instead project number EA 398 was initiated and would eventually become the Scirocco. The intention, even at that stage was to share as many components as possible with the forthcoming Beetle replacement.

Giugiaro's first proposal, based on the 1600 Beetle, was called the Volkswagen Karmann Cheetah and signalled the start of the designer's wedge period. This prototype roadster had some unique features. Instead of a traditional roll bar, two B pillars joined up to the door frame and windscreen creating a cage. This meant that the

hard and soft top arrangements were greatly simplified. At the front, there was a soft rubber nose and retractable headlights. If this all sounds and maybe looks slightly familiar, then perhaps the arrival a year later of the Bertone X1/9 styled by Marcello Gandini is not a coincidence. The influence has never been officially acknowledged, but it is pretty obvious. Volkswagen, though, were not interested in the Cheetah as the problems for Volkswagen President Kurt Lotz mounted.

Giugiaro decided to take matters into his own hands. As Rudolf Leidling assumed control at Volkswagen, the Italian designer went direct to Karmann with his revised proposal to create a new 2+2 coupé on the short Golf wheelbase. Karmann felt strongly enough about the car to present the project officially to Wolfsburg, who ultimately

This is EA 398 – the 1970 Karmann Cheetah and eventually the Scirocco. Styled by Guigiaro, it was Beetle 1600 based, although the intention was that it would have the future Golf's running gear.

pleaded poverty. So the Scirocco was largely financed by Karmann who were con-
tracted for body pressing, welding, paint-
ing and final assembly. For their part
Volkswagen became more closely involved
with the engineering side than at any time
since the old Karmann Ghia days.

SCIROCCO – A FRESH WIND

The resulting sports car was simple and
perfectly proportioned. As with many of his
designs it is possible to see how Giugiaro
arrived at the final shape by looking at his
contemporary portfolio. Karmann had
asked Italdesign to come up with a coupé
for the 1973 Frankfurt Motor Show. Based
on the Audi 80, the Asso Di Picche shared
the uncluttered side elevation of the

Scirocco with a raked rear windscreen at
the back and an almost identical, narrow
four headlamp grille at the front. One similar car that did make it to production was
the Alfa Romeo Alfetta – launched at the
same time but quite clearly an earlier, softer design. The long gestation period from
1969 explains this. Otherwise the basic
shape is broadly similar, yet the Scirocco
looks far more taut and tidy.

The distinctive wrap-around tailgate
was first revealed to the public on the
Scirocco although it was an original feature
of the Golf. The tailgate itself also featured
a small spoiler-like lip, and the rear light
clusters were large and well proportioned
as Giugiaro had intended for the Golf
before being overruled on cost grounds. Up
front it was the new corporate look, with a
full width grille, silver Volkswagen roundel

*The first clue as to how the Scirocco might look was this 1973 Karmann proposal based on an Audi
80, itself a close relative of the future Golf and Scirocco.*

and (on European specification models) four headlamps. Karmann were so happy with the result that they presented Giugiaro with a Scirocco. This was the first time that the designer had been given one of his own creations.

The Scirocco went into production before the Golf, so that any difficulties that might affect the similar and more important family model could be resolved early. It was launched at the 1974 Geneva Motor Show and there were four models available. The basic L model was powered by a 1,093cc engine producing 50bhp or a 70bhp

A base specification German Scirocco with rectangular headlamps.

Inside a 1974 Scirocco.

Scirocco GLi and GTi 1600

Engine

	Four cylinder in line, toothed belt driven SOHC
	Alloy cylinder head, cast iron block transversely mounted in front
	Bosch K-Jetronic fuel injection
Capacity	1,588cc
Bore	79.5 × 80mm
Output	110bhp at 6100rpm
Compression ratio	9.5:1
Maximum torque	102.9lb/ft at 5000rpm

Transmission

	Front wheel drive
4-speed all synchromesh	3.46, 1.94, 1.37, 0.97:1
Reverse	3.27:1
Final drive	3.7:1
5-speed	3.45, 2.12, 1.44, 1.13, 0.91:1
Reverse	3.17:1
Final drive	3.9:1

Suspension

Front	Independent with MacPherson struts, lower wishbones, coil springs and anti-roll bar
Rear	Semi-independent with trailing arms, torsion beam, coil springs, telescopic dampers and anti-roll bar

Steering

	Rack and pinion
	3.3 turns lock to lock

Tyres and wheels

175/70HR-13 on 5.5J × 13

Dimensions

Track – front	55.3in (1,405mm)
Track – rear	54in (1,372mm)
Wheelbase	94.5in (2,400mm)
Length	151.8in (3,855mm)
Width	64in (1,625mm)
Height	51.6in (1,310mm)
Unladen weight	1,762lb (800kg)

Performance

Top speed	115mph (185kph)
Acceleration	0–60mph in 9.0 seconds

Fuel consumption

Touring	29mpg (9.7 litres per 100km)

1,471cc. Reclining seats, two-speed wipers, electric windscreen washers and a clock were standard equipment. The higher specification TS and LS models came with the 1.5 engine in a 85bhp state of tune. In most markets a heated rear window, cigarette lighter, arm-rests and carpeting were all part of the package; the range topping LS had a distinctive four headlamp grille. The interior mirrored the Golf, but there was a three-spoke sports steering wheel.

The Scirocco received its first mechanical upgrade in autumn 1975 when the 1.5 unit was replaced by a 75bhp, 1,588cc engine, with low (8.2:1) and high (9.7:1) compression versions for the low and high specification models. It got hotter a year later when the fuel injected 1.6 engine from the Golf GTI was fitted to two new

models: a GTI and more highly trimmed GLi. Carburettor versions of these were also available in some markets badged as GT and GL. At the same time out went the conventional twin windscreen wipers to be replaced by a single arm, an arrangement that was destined to become fashionable. The ventilation system was improved with a 3-speed blower.

A major facelift year for the Scirocco arrived in 1977. Front and rear ends were tidied up, and heavy duty bumpers and four headlamps across the range changed the outward appearance. The dreadful clown's trousers interior upholstery was toned down and the seats with their integral headrests were replaced by Golf type sports seats. Mechanically there were more options as a shorter stroke 1,588cc engine

First Scirocco facelift in line with the Golf as it gets bigger wrap-around bumpers in 1977.

The original Scirocco Storm, sold only in the UK. It had a colour keyed spoiler, metallic paint and leather interior. The best of the early models.

was introduced, rated at 1,457cc and producing 70bhp. A GLS version with uprated equipment and trim, including alloy wheels, velour upholstery and metallic paint now topped the range.

In 1979 the 1,093cc unit in the basic models was replaced by a 1,272cc that produced 60bhp. At the same time, 5-speed gearboxes became standard on the GLI and optional on the other models. In the UK, the GTi was finally imported with a standard 5-speed gearbox. It was joined by a special edition Storm, which came with a very high specification including special metallic colours – silver green or black with either black or fawn leather upholstery. The Storm proved popular and was reintroduced in 1981 to help sell the last of the old shape models. It was then available in silver, blue or brown, with blue or tan leather upholstery, and alloy wheels last seen on the Passat.

SCIROCCO REBORN

Herbert Schäfer, who ran the newly creat-

ed design studio at Wolfsburg, was not the biggest fan of Giugiaro's original Scirocco. Perhaps that explains why the Italian designer had no hand in the revised model. Giugiaro had begun producing updates of the original shape in league with Karmann since 1977. Of the five designs shortlisted, two were Giugiaro's although they remained anonymous while the decision was made. Certainly the winning in-house proposal owed much to earlier works by Italdesign. (Many pointed to a couple of Karmann show cars from the late 1970s. The 'Ace of Diamonds' was built on a BMW 3 series chassis and proposed a smaller companion to the 6 series coupé. Its closeness to the Scirocco meant that it came to nothing. The 'Ace of Clubs', which used a rear wheel drive Isuzu Gemini chassis, turned into the Isuzu Piazza.)

SCIROCCO GOES XL

For some, the re-bodied Scirocco of 1981 lost some of the purity of the original Giugiaro design. Some of the sharpness

A 1977 suggestion from Karmann and Giugiaro as to how the next generation Scirocco should look. Volkswagen did not take up the invitation, but were clearly heavily influenced by the shape when it came to styling the Mark 2 in-house.

The re-bodied Scirocco, more aerodynamic and better accommodation.

may have gone, with softer, more aerodynamic lines – drag coefficient down from 0.42 to 0.38 – while the repositioning of rear spoiler reduced rear end lift by a massive 60 per cent, but on the inside there were some signs of relief. There was 0.4in (10mm) more headroom at the front, and back seat passengers had a massive 0.7in (18mm) extra to play with, plus more elbow and leg room. Over half of the extra length of 6.7in (165mm) was put to good use in the boot as the capacity went up by 20 per cent.

The model line-up comprised L, LS, GL, GT and GTI. The L was powered by the 1,272cc engine, or 1,457cc when it was badged LS. A GL with rev counter, clock and sports steering wheel with additional halogen headlamps was available with both the smaller units and an 85bhp version of the 1,588cc engine. The GT came with the 1.5 and 1.6 engines and was distinguished by a huge Scirocco logo emblazoned on the rear window and four rectangular headlamps at the front. Specification included sports seats, temperature gauge and split rear shelf. The GTi mirrored the specification of its hatchback cousin with a 110bhp fuel injected 1.6 engine, close ratio gearbox, uprated suspension and rear anti-roll bar.

In September 1982 there was a wholesale engine change, uprated in line with the hatchback with the new 1.8, producing 112bhp. There were also several engine changes across the rest of the Scirocco range as the 1.5 was replaced by a new 1,595cc unit producing 75bhp. That resulted in the 1,588cc carburettor being superseded by a 90bhp version of the 1,781cc engine. As well as the Scirocco switching to a twin windscreen wiper system the range was re-designated CL, GL, GT, GLi and GTi.

RADICAL SCIROCCOS

Volkswagen engineers seriously considered using a turbocharger to boost the performance of all their GTI models. Tests began in 1981 with the 1.6 engine but it was found that an uncomfortable amount of heat was generated, while fuel consumption proved to be very poor indeed. They tried again in 1983 with an American specification 1.7 litre engine that produced an impressive 178bhp resulting in 138mph (222kph) top speed. However, development of the 16-valve head scuppered the turbo and showed that Volkswagen were taking the multi-valve performance route.

Probably the most radical Scirocco of all was the twin engined beast developed by the Motorsport Department. They used two bored out (to 1,791cc) and tuned versions of the 1.6 unit, which each produced 180bhp. It showed up the sister companies Audi Quattro Sport in terms of power and potential abilities yet was never homologated. However, Volkswagen went so far as to put it into production when the Development Department got involved. In 1984 they took the Scirocco to the high performance extreme by using two Oettinger-tuned 16-valve 141bhp engines. Despite the attractively blistered arches, very Quattro, no green light was given for homologation.

STORM AND 16 VALVES

In 1984 the Storm was back, this time with a Zender body kit, 6J × 14in alloy wheels and 185/60VR-14 tyres. Cosmetically, buyers could choose from metallic blue or brown, with blue or beige interior plus leather covered steering wheel rim, gaiter and gear knob. GTX models that arrived at the same time to replace the GTi also aped the Storm style with the Zender body kit

The Scirocco Turbo was sidelined by the arrival of the 16-valve.

The amazingly powerful Bimotor Scirocco.

Scirocco 2 1.8 GTI/GTX

Engine

Four cylinder in line, toothed belt driven SOHC
Alloy cylinder head, cast iron block transversely mounted in front
Bosch K-Jetronic fuel injection

Capacity	1,781cc
Bore	81 × 86.4mm
Output	112bhp at 5800rpm
Compression ratio	10.0:1
Maximum torque	109lb/ft at 3500rpm

Transmission

Front wheel drive

5-speed	3.45, 2.18, 1.44, 1.13, 0.91:1
Reverse	3.17:1
Final drive	3.67:1

Suspension

Front	Independent with MacPherson struts, lower wishbones, coil springs and anti-roll bar
Rear	Semi-independent with trailing arms, torsion beam, coil springs, telescopic dampers and anti-roll bar

Steering

Rack and pinion
3.7 turns lock to lock (power option 3.2)

Brakes

9.4in (239mm) ventilated front discs, 8.9in (226mm) solid rear discs
Vacuum servo

Tyres and wheels

175/70HR-13 on 5.5 × 13

Dimensions

Track – front	55.3in (1,405mm)
Track – rear	53.9in (1,370mm)
Wheelbase	94.5in (2,400mm)
Length	159.4in (4,050mm)
Width	64in (1,625mm)
Height	51.4in (1,305mm)
Unladen weight	2,026lb (920kg)

Performance

Top speed	117mph (188kph)
Acceleration	0–60mph in 9.4 seconds

Fuel consumption

Overall	30mpg (9.4 litres per 100km)

and similar interior trimmings. In addition, alloy wheels, sunroof, central locking, trip computer and tinted glass completed the standard specification.

The launch of the 16-valve Scirocco in June 1985 meant that it became a coupé to take very seriously indeed. All of a sudden 130mph (209kph) and 0–60mph in 7.6

The second Storm, this time with a Zender body kit.

A 16-valve on the track.

seconds became possible. Apart from the engine transplant there were other upgrades that included a larger exhaust, stronger drive shafts and a larger 12.1 gallon (55 litre) fuel tank. In the brake department there were rear discs for the first time and the front discs were ventilated. Suspension was beefed up with an extra brace on the front wishbones, stiffer springs, anti-roll bars and revised settings for the shock absorbers.

SCIROCCO SWAN SONG

In 1988 the range was re-vamped for the UK market and rationalized down to three models: a 1.6 GT, 1.8 GTX and in the middle

---

Scirocco 16V GTX

Engine

Four cylinder in line, toothed belt driven SOHC
Alloy cylinder head, cast iron block transversely mounted in front
Bosch K-Jetronic fuel injection

Capacity	1,781cc
Bore	81 × 86.4mm
Output	139bhp at 6100rpm
Compression ratio	10.0:1
Maximum torque	133lb/ft at 4600rpm

Transmission

Front wheel drive

5-speed	3.45, 2.18, 1.44, 1.13, 0.91:1
Reverse	3.17:1
Final drive	3.67:1

Suspension

Front	Independent with MacPherson struts, lower wishbones, coil springs anti-roll bar
Rear	Semi-independent with trailing arms, torsion beam, coil springs, telescopic dampers and anti-roll bar

Steering

Rack and pinion
3.7 turns lock to lock (power option 3.2)

Brakes

9.4in (239mm) ventilated front discs, 8.9in (226mm) rear discs
Vacuum servo

Tyres and wheels

175/70HR-13 on 5.5 × 13

Dimensions

Track – front	55.3in (1,405mm)
Track – rear	53.9in (1,370mm)
Wheelbase	94.5in (2,400mm)
Length	159.4in (4,050mm)
Width	64in (1,625mm)
Height	51.4in (1,305mm)
Unladen weight	2,643lb (1,200kg)

Performance

Top speed	130mph (209kph)
Acceleration	0–60mph in 7.8 seconds

Fuel consumption

Overall	27mpg (10.4 litres per 100km)

a 1.8 carburettor fed Scala. The 8-valve line-up of engines in all world markets now comprised the 75bhp 1.6, a catalysed 72bhp version, a 90bhp 1.8, an injected 112bhp and a catalysed/Lambda probe equipped American specification version with hydraulic tappets. On the 16-valve front there were two versions already fitted to the Golf and Jetta models. There was the standard 139bhp version and a catalyst equipped 16-valve unit producing 129bhp.

Although 1989 saw the introduction of the Corrado, the Scirocco gamely soldiered on, although the range was heavily rationalized. In the UK buyers could choose between a 90bhp GT and a fuel injected Scala. On the Continent only a 72bhp 1.6 and 95bhp 1.8 were available as the 16-valve was quietly phased out.

The Scirocco was laid to rest in July 1992 when the last example rolled off the Karmann production line. The final models were badged either Scala or GT II and had colour keyed paintwork and revised interiors. They were offered with 95 or 129bhp versions of the 1.8 engine. They closed a remarkable period in the life of one of the most enduring and successful European 2+2 coupés ever. Almost 800,000 had been

sold over a seventeen year period.

CORRADO – SEARCHING FOR A SUPER COUPÉ

Before coming up with the very original hot hatch concept in 1976 and steadily warming over the Scirocco, Volkswagen had always cherished the idea of producing a proper performance sports car. That is why the all new Corrado was not intended as a direct replacement for the relatively tame 2+2 Scirocco coupé.

The previous false starts occurred first in 1969 when Volkswagen linked up with Porsche to produce the 914. Badged as a Porsche in America and a Volkswagen in Europe, even the 916, with the addition of a flat six from a 911, could not revive the model's flagging fortunes. Volkswagen tried again with their old pals Porsche, but got cold feet as the early 1970s energy crisis deepened. As a result the project was farmed out to another part of the group, Audi, who built the highly successful 924 for Porsche.

In the late 1980s production of the 924 was coming to an end, there was a 2+2

The Corrado G60

revival among European manufacturers and increasing quantities of high performance coupés were coming from the Far East. Volkswagen did not want to miss out on this burgeoning market. They came up with a shape that took plenty of cues from the Scirocco, with minimal rear overhang and a kicked up rear window. The Corrado name was not related to anything meteorological for a change – it came from the Spanish verb 'correr', meaning to run or race. Although Golf based, the new car weighed 400lb (182kg) more, which hardly helped the acceleration figures, but the top speed improved because of the superior aerodynamics. It shared front MacPherson strut and wishbone suspension with the GTI. However, at the back was a revised torsion beam system first used on the new style Passat, which effectively added an element of rear wheel steer.

The Passat also donated its 5-speed gearbox combined with a 3.45:1 final drive ratio. This was connected to a supercharged 1.8 litre engine that produced 160bhp and the car was badged a G60. A special 16-valve model was made solely for the UK and Italian markets. Power steering was standard but there were variations when it came to brakes. ABS by Teves was standard on the G60, which had 11.4in (280mm) front discs, while the 16-valve made do with 10.4in (256mm) diameter ones. Underneath, 6.5 × 15in BBS cross-spoke alloy wheels with 195/50VR-15 tyres were the order of the day on the G60 while the 16-valve made do with 6Js and 185/55VR-15 tyres. The standard package was not over-generous – buyers got green tinted glass and a computer but everything else had to be ordered from the options list.

Inside, the Corrado was quite different

Corrado 16V 1.8

Engine

	Four cylinder in line, toothed belt driven SOHC
	Alloy cylinder head, cast iron block transversely mounted in front
	Bosch K-Jetronic fuel injection
Capacity	1,781cc
Bore	81 × 86.4mm
Output	136bhp at 6300rpm
Compression ratio	10.0:1
Maximum torque	119lb/ft at 4800rpm

Transmission

	Front wheel drive
5-speed	3.40, 2.12, 1.44, 1.13, 0.91:1 (3.78, 2.21, 1.43, 1.03, 0.84:1 from 1992)
Reverse	3.80:1
Final drive	3.68:1

Suspension

Front	Independent with MacPherson struts, lower wishbones, coil springs and anti-roll bar
Rear	Semi-independent with trailing arms and track correcting bearings, torsion beam, coil springs, and anti-roll bar

Steering

Rack and pinion
3.17 turns lock to lock

Brakes

10in (254mm) ventilated front discs
10in (254mm) rear discs
ABS standard

Tyres and wheels

195/50VR-15 on 6 × 15

Dimensions

Track – front   56.5in (1,435mm)
Track – rear   56.3in (1,430mm)
Wheelbase   97.2in (2,470mm)
Length   159.4in (4,050mm)
Width   65.7in (1,670mm)
Height   52in (1,320mm)
Unladen weight   2,423lb (1,100kg)

Performance

Top speed   131mph (211kph)
Acceleration   0–60mph in 8.7 seconds

Fuel consumption

Overall   29 to 31mpg (9.1 to 9.7 litres per 100km)

Corrado 16V 2.0
Engine

Four cylinder in line, toothed belt driven SOHC
Alloy cylinder head, cast iron block transversely mounted in front
Bosch K-Jetronic fuel injection

Capacity   1,984cc
Bore   82.5 × 92.8mm
Output   136bhp at 5800rpm
Compression ratio 10.8:1
Maximum torque   132lb/ft at 4400rpm

Transmission

Front wheel drive

5-speed   3.40, 2.12, 1.44, 1.13, 0.91:1 (3.78, 2.21, 1.43, 1.03, 0.84:1 from 1992)
Reverse   3.80:1
Final drive   3.68:1

Suspension

Front   Independent with MacPherson struts, lower wishbones, coil springs
                   and anti-roll bar

Rear	Semi-independent with trailing arms and track correcting bearings, torsion beam, coil springs, and anti-roll bar

Steering

	Rack and pinion
	3.17 turns lock to lock

Brakes

	10in (254mm) ventilated front discs
	10in (254mm) rear discs
	ABS standard

Tyres and wheels

	195/50VR-15 on 6 × 15

Dimensions

Track – front	56.5in (1,435mm)
Track – rear	56.3in (1,430mm)
Wheelbase	97.2in (2,470mm)
Length	159.4in (4,050mm)
Width	65.7in (1,670mm)
Height	52in (1,320mm)
Unladen weight	2,423lb (1,100kg)

Performance

Top speed	126mph (203kph)
Acceleration	0–60mph in 10.2 seconds

Fuel consumption

Overall	29 to 31mpg (9.1 to 9.7 litres per 100km)

from the Mark 2 Golfs. In the centre were three large dials, set in a large smoothly styled dashboard that hinted at future Golf layouts. It was a close relative of the Passat, while the 100 per cent plastic steering wheel started life in a poverty specification Golf. The plastic moulded door trims were downright tacky. The seat trim material was a low key tartan and, where specified, leather. Like the Scirocco, the Corrado was a 2+2, but back seat passengers felt a little more claustrophobic thanks to the high tail.

The rear seat was divided in two with a centre arm-rest that also contained a first aid kit, while a pocket in the top of the back-rest accommodated a warning triangle. And that was not all that the rear seat could do – there was a 60/40 split that could boost the original 10.5cu ft (297 litres) of luggage space to an impressive 29.4cu ft (833 litres) with the squabs folded forward. To help the driver's already restricted rear vision there was a final trick in the tail as the rear spoiler could raise itself by 2in (50mm) once a pre set speed – between 45 and 75mph (72 and 121kph) according to the market – was reached. It was not just a gimmick because Volkswagen reckoned that the extra downforce created by the extended airfoil amounted to 64 per cent.

Inside the Corrado.

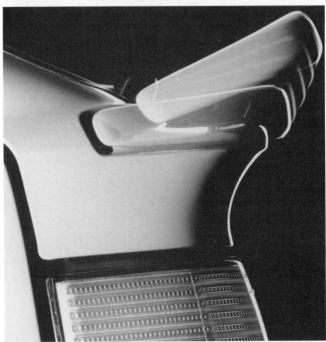

*The Corrado's trick spoiler, which rose
automatically when the car reached a
set speed.*

CORRADO IN ACTION

The G60 turned out to be a great car, and its power and acceleration won plenty of converts. The old GTI engine could propel this 2,453lb (1,114kg) lightweight to 140mph (225kph). What might bother the sensitive, though, was the constant hum of the supercharger. Handling was a depart- ment where Volkswagen always excelled and the Corrado was no exception. Like the Golf it would tuck up a rear wheel at speed, but this would never upset the car's balance. Tremendous grip, traction, responsive steering and directional stability added up to a safe, yet invigorating drive. On a purely practical level, the small Corrado offered plenty of room

---

Corrado G60

Engine

	Four cylinder in line, toothed belt driven SOHC
	Alloy cylinder head, cast iron block transversely mounted in front
	Double belt driven G-Lader supercharger running at 1.6 times engine speed
	Intercooler
	Digifant fuel injection
Capacity	1,781cc
Bore	81 × 86.4mm
Output	60bhp at 5600rpm
Compression ratio	8:1
Maximum torque	165lb/ft at 4000rpm

Transmission

	Front wheel drive
5-speed	3.78, 2.12, 1.34, 0.97, 0.76:1
Reverse	3.80:1
Final drive	3.67:1

Suspension

Front	Independent with MacPherson struts, lower wishbones, coil springs and anti-roll bar
Rear	Semi-independent with trailing arms and track correcting bearings, torsion beam, coil springs, and anti-roll bar

Steering

	Rack and pinion
	3.17 turns lock to lock

Brakes

	11in (280mm) ventilated front discs, 8.9in (226mm) rear discs
	ABS standard

Tyres and wheels

	195/50VR-15 on 6 × 15

Dimensions

Track – front	56.5in (1,435mm)
Track – rear	56.3in (1,430mm)
Wheelbase	97.2in (2,470mm)
Length	159.4in (4,050mm)
Width	65.7in (1,670mm)
Height	52in (1,320mm)
Unladen weight	2,456lb (1,115kg)

Performance

Top speed	137mph (220kph)
Acceleration	0–60mph in 8.9 seconds

Fuel consumption

Overall	22mpg (12.8 litres per 100km)

inside. There was a lot of stowage space in the door pockets, a reasonable amount of room for two rear seat passengers, especially for their heads, all tailed off with an impressively deep boot. The seats were comfortable and the driving position just about perfect, an adjustable steering column being crucial to sitting comfortably. There was criticism of the cable operated Passat gearbox, which could feel vague – hardly an appropriate choice for a sports car. The 12 gallon (54.6 litre) fuel tank was a mere apology for a petrol reservoir. Inside, the Passat dashboard disappointed and it was not a place for the claustrophobic. Those traditional Golf C pillars and a high waistline made it a dark place to be.

Despite all that, *Car* in January 1989 pronounced it one of the best coupés of its kind as it outclassed much more expensive rivals in the shape of the Audi Coupé Quattro and Porsche 944 in their giant test. Just six months later another test in the magazine indicated just how fast the competition from the Far East was catching up. The Corrado was squeezed out of first place by the incredibly quick Nissan 200SX, while the Toyota Celica GT and

Honda Prelude were close behind.

By May 1992 *Car* concluded that it was all over for the Corrado as both the Honda Prelude 2.3 and Mazda MX-6 made the Volkswagen seem just a little old fashioned. 'Time and technology have caught up with the G60' they said. The Corrado amused the road testers and snared their affections, but sadly it could not better the Japanese models in any way.

CORRADO UPGRADES

Volkswagen were quickly aware that the standard specification had to be upgraded, so within a year electric windows, central locking, height-adjustable steering column and a radio/cassette with nifty speed related volume control was part of the package. Fetishists could thrill to the leather covered steering wheel and gear knob, plus hide trimmings on the gear lever and hand brake gaiters.

The first major model update occurred for the 1992 model year. The exterior facelift amounted to a new four bar grille. Up went the fuel tank capacity from 12.1

Here is a Corrado G60 without its roof. Karmann did this in 1995 to show what could be done to make a very attractive high performance convertible. Shame it never went into production.

gallons (55 litres) to 15.4 gallons (69 litres). The radio/cassette was of the pull out variety, the intermittent screen wipe had an adjustable delay and a torch key illuminated the way. Most improvements came the way of the 16-valve model. Under the bonnet it received the new 1,984cc engine from the Mark 3 Golf, catalyst equipped with K-Motronic fuel injection. Output remained at 136bhp, although the torque was significantly improved at 132lb/ft at 4,400rpm. There was criticism of the inappropriate gear ratios, which contributed to less than smooth engine performance. ABS was now standard, along with 6J × 15in Estoril alloy wheels, and inside new Domino trim made a visual difference.

For 1993 there were more interior changes as the electric window switches were repositioned and there were major changes to indicator stalks, air vents and new rotary heater controls. The finishing touch was neat red instrument needles. After that, the biggest news was chrome rather than body colour badging in late 1993.

In 1994 Volkswagen introduced an entry level Corrado powered by the 8-valve 2.0 litre engine used in the GTI. Electric windows, mirrors, green tinted glass, alloy wheels, rear wash/wipe, alloy wheels, front fog lamps and sports seats were all part of the package.

CORRADO VR6

The ultimate Corrado arrived in 1992 when the 2,861cc V6 engine first seen in 2,792cc form powering the Golf VR6 was installed in it. This truly stunning coupé produced 190bhp at 5,800rpm, powered to 60mph in just 6.4 seconds and the top speed was 145mph (233kph). The big problem was getting the front wheels to cope with all that power, so Volkswagen arranged for the brakes to be applied automatically if one wheel turned faster than the other.

Corrado VR6

Engine

	15-degree V6 cylinder SOHC
	Alloy cylinder head, cast iron block transversely mounted in front
	Bosch Motronic fuel injection
Capacity	2,861cc
Bore	82 × 90.3mm
Output	190bhp at 5800rpm
Compression ratio	10:1
Maximum torque	181lb/ft at 4200rpm

Transmission

	Front wheel drive
5-speed	3.78, 2.12, 1.46, 1.03, 0.84:1
Reverse	3.39:
Final drive	3.67:1

Suspension

| Front | Independent with MacPherson struts, lower wishbones, coil springs and anti-roll bar |
| Rear | Semi-independent with trailing arms and track correcting bearings, torsion beam, coil springs, and anti-roll bar |

Steering

Rack and pinion, 3.17 turns lock to lock

Brakes

11in (280mm) ventilated front discs, 8.9in (226mm) rear discs
ABS
Electronic traction control linked to front brakes

Tyres and wheels

205/50R-15V on 6.5 × 15

Dimensions

Track – front	56.5in (1,435mm)
Track – rear	56.3in (1,430mm)
Wheelbase	97.2in (2,470mm)
Length	159.4in (4,050mm)
Width	65.7in (1,670mm)
Height	52in (1,320mm)
Unladen weight	2,731lb (1,240kg)

Performance

Top speed	144mph (232kph)
Acceleration	0–60mph in 7.2 seconds

Fuel consumption

Overall	25mpg (11.3 litres per 100km)

Corrado VR6, quite simply the quickest Volkswagen ever.

An easy car to drive, the VR6 pulled well at low revs with little need for progressive gear changes. Easy and almost friendly, it turned into corners smoothly and safely. However hard the driver went, the VR6 maintained its poise. Undoubtedly the rear torsion beam suspension with track correcting mounts meant that even an inept driver who backed off had trouble unsettling the rear end. Accelerate hard though and the VR6 would widen its line in a neat outward drift. That finesse always made the Corrado, and the VR6 in particular, very rewarding to drive.

CORRADO CANCELLED

By 1995 Volkswagen had done their sums and found that the Corrado was not paying its way. Models from the Far East had made big worldwide inroads into the coupé market, a market that had begun to go off the boil. Sadly, Volkswagen decided to bow out and at the time of writing there are only rumours that they will return.

To reward their most loyal and appreciative customers, Volkswagen made sure that the very last Corrado models to leave the production line were 500 right hand drive VR6 Storm models bound for the UK. Mechanically they were no different from the standard VR6. From the outside the main Storm give-away was the colour: just two were offered, Mystic Blue and Classic Green, which were both pearl effect metallic finishes. The blue Storm had a black leather interior, the green had light beige. The other distinctive feature was the Solitude alloy wheels, the same size 6.5 ×

It is fitting that the last ever Corrado should not just create a Storm, but be called one too. Just like the best of the limited edition Sciroccos this VR6 special is set to become a collector's item.

15in as the standard Corrado wheels. Apart from the 'Storm' badges the only specification upgrades were front seat heating and an upgraded Sony radio and CD player.

Could this be the end of Volkswagen's coupé era? In 1993 the Corrado replacement was put on ice, although it has been rumoured that the Polo floor pan may be used for a less ambitious 2-door model.

9 Golf Open – The Karmann Convertibles

'Volkswagen has given new meaning to the term German Open' – Volkswagen press release.

Just as the Beetle was the most successful production vehicle of its day, the Karmann convertible consistently broke production records during its long life. From 1949 until 1975 it was the most successful soft top ever. By 1978 a world record production figure of 331,426 had been reached. Clearly there was a market for a sensibly sized convertible that was neither a tiny sports car nor an opulent oversized roadster. With the Beetle gone and the marginally more sporting Karmann Ghia discontinued the way was clear for a rival, or a Volkswagen based replacement.

There were strong rumours that American safety regulations would

Two generations of Karmann Golf convertibles. Practical, solid and always stylish.

effectively ban open topped cars. Old Volks-wagen collaborators Karmann were once again wielding the cutting equipment and were smart enough to set about building one of the most rigid convertibles on the market with its distinctive roll bar. This enabled the car to sail through the strict rollover test for saloons as described in United States Federal Motor Vehicle Safety Standard 208.

SOFT TOP, TOUGH UNDERNEATH

Like the Scirocco, the new convertible was based on the floor pan of the Mark 1 Golf, but such a conversion was hardly a straightforward project. Take away the roof section of a car, especially a model as rigid and strong as the Golf, and all that

holds the two ends together is the floor pan. Reinforcements are therefore needed, so Karmann specified a substantial roll bar, which provided anchorage points for the seat belts and guide channels for the door glass and rear windows. At the front an additional cross-beam beefed up the area behind the dashboard and the suspension turrets were also reinforced. Further back, the sills were strengthened between the wheel arches, there was a box section cross-beam mounted behind the rear seats and a boxed boot structure. Not surprisingly, the weight went up by 300lb (136kg) over the standard car.

The boot area would always be a compromise. Karmann wanted to bury the hood structure neatly into the rear deck; Volkswagen insisted on a decently sized boot. In fact, the fold-forward rear seat and removable parcel shelf meant that there

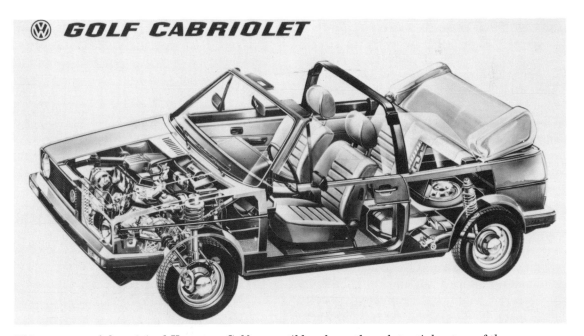

This cutaway of the original Karmann Golf convertibles shows the substantial nature of the construction and the importance of that roll bar.

This is Karmann's 1976 prototype convertible with a neat rear deck and the hood stowed largely in the boot area. Rearward vision was excellent. However, Volkswagen specified a bigger boot and did not mind the higher hood.

was plenty more room in the cockpit for larger items, and the hood always made the car look like a pram. It was a substantial structure, comprising a complex steel framework covered with multi-layer fabrics and incorporating a glass rear screen – no more flimsy plastic screens leading to fogging, tearing and misery. With the hood up it was easy to believe that you were travelling inside a normal tin top Golf; it was snug and comfortable. Rear passengers however, did not feel the same way. For a start they had 2in (50mm) less elbow room compared with the hatchback. In addition, once the hood was lowered – by releasing two catches at the top of the windscreen and then lowering it to the deck with the assistance of two pneumatic struts – rear seat passengers had to endure a fair amount of buffeting from the wind. Getting out of the back also meant avoiding the hefty roll bar. But those were the only minor gripes in an otherwise perfect package.

The convertible made its debut at the Geneva Motor Show in 1979 and was offered in most markets as a GLi, which meant the 1,588cc GTI engine and suspension modifications, and a GLS with better trim but a 70bhp 1,457cc engine. There was no competition at all for the open topped Golf. Like the GTI, which rewrote the sports car rule book, the convertible was a further blow to the prehistoric yet traditional Triumphs and MGs. Volkswagen proved that a car could be fast and practical without any compromises and revived the old fashioned cabriolet, seating four in relative comfort. The Golf convertible inspired manufacturers to raise the roof on their hatchbacks – but Volkswagen had a head start.

THE CONSISTENT CONVERTIBLE

Over the years the modifications ran parallel to the hatchbacks when in 1982 the 1.8 litre GTI engine was installed into

Three views of the new convertibles in GLS trim. Once erected the substantial hood was as snug as a hardtop. Folding it away was always quick and straightforward.

the GLi and the 1,457cc unit was replaced by the 1,595cc carburettor unit in 1983. The fascia was given a facelift along with the hatchbacks in 1981 to include a lockable glove box and centre console, and the body hugging sports seats became part of the standard specification in 1983. What did stay exactly the same throughout the life of the Karmann cabriolet, however, was the bodywork. The Mark 1 shape stayed,

but that did not stop the angular lines from starting to date. So in 1988 there was a concerted attempt to soften up the bodywork by adding new smoother moulded bumpers, an integrated front spoiler and rear apron. Sill and wheel arch extensions were incorporated in the design.

By 1985 the GTI designation was finally adopted for UK specification convertibles, and a 1.6 GL model with optional automatic

Karmann proposed a Jetta convertible and came up with this very accomplished convertible that looked just right for production. Volkswagen, however, were happy with the Golf and saw no point having both models competing for the same customers – so it was never taken any further.

Softer bodies from 1988 as the bumpers were rounded off and a new still panel was integrated into the wheel arch extensions. Colour keying helped the effect of this Clipper model that replaced the GL and was powered by a carburettor version of the 1.8 unit.

and 4+E gearboxes also appeared. There were twin headlamp grilles, re-styled 'sports' rear seats, a rev counter on the GL and the on-board computer as fitted to the GTI. The 1988 bodywork upgrades also saw the introduction of the Clipper with 1.8 carburettor power replacing the GL. Equipment levels increased in 1990 to keep

Mark 1 Golf Karmann 1987 (Clipper)

Engine

Four cylinder in line, toothed belt driven SOHC
Alloy cylinder head, cast iron block transversely mounted in front

Capacity	1,781cc
Bore	81.0 × 86.4mm
Output	90bhp at 5200rpm
Compression ratio	10.0:1
Maximum torque	107lb/ft at 3300rpm

Transmission

Front wheel drive
4-speed all synchromesh

Suspension

Front	Independent with MacPherson struts, lower wishbones, coil springs
Rear	Semi-independent with trailing arms, torsion beam, coil springs, telescopic dampers

Steering

Rack and pinion
3.3 turns lock to lock

Brakes

9.4in (239mm) front discs, 8.9in (226mm) rear drums
Vacuum servo

Dimensions

Track – front	55.3in (1,404mm)
Track – rear	54in (1,372mm)
Wheelbase	94.5in (2,400mm)
Length	150.2in (3,815mm)
Width	64.2in (1,630mm)
Height	54.9in (1,395mm)
Ground clearance	4.6in (117mm)
Unladen weight	208,3.8lb (946.0kg)

Performance

Top speed	106mph (171kph)
Acceleration	0–60mph in 10.5 seconds

Fuel consumption

30.0mpg (9.4 litres per 100km)

up with other manufacturers who had entered this burgeoning market. Apart from radio upgrades the most significant addition to the GTI model was an electro-

hydraulically operated hood. This made life easier as all the driver had to do was release the securing catches and then press a button.

GLi and GTI 1.8

Engine

Four cylinder in line, toothed belt driven SOHC
Alloy cylinder head, cast iron block transversely mounted in front
Bosch K-Jetronic fuel injection

Capacity	1,781cc
Bore	81 × 86.4mm
Output	112bhp at 5800rpm
Compression ratio	10.0:1
Maximum torque	109lb/ft at 3500rpm

Transmission

Front wheel drive

5-speed	3.45, 2.12, 1.44, 1.13, 0.91:1
Reverse	3.17:1
Final drive	3.895:1

Suspension

Front	Independent with MacPherson struts, lower wishbones, coil springs and anti-roll bar
Rear	Semi-independent with trailing arms, torsion beam, coil springs, telescopic dampers and anti-roll bar

Steering

Rack and pinion
3.3 turns lock to lock

Brakes

9.4in (239mm) ventilated front discs, 8.9in (226mm) rear drums
Vacuum servo

Tyres and wheels

175/70HR-13 on 5.5J × 13

Dimensions

Track – front	55.3in (1,405mm)
Track – rear	54in (1,372mm)
Wheelbase	94.5in (2,400mm)
Length (1979–83)	150.2in (3,815mm)
Length (1983–93)	150.8in (3,830mm)
Width	64.1in (1,628mm)
Height	54.9in (1,395mm)
Unladen weight	2,070lb (940kg)

Performance	
Top speed	111mph (179kph)
Acceleration	0–60mph in 9.8 seconds
Fuel consumption	
Constant 75mph (121kph)	36.5mpg (7.7 litres per 100km)

With the arrival of the Mark 2 Golf in 1983 it was expected that a Karmann convertible would follow in due course. It did not. The cost of developing and building a niche model where production and sales are limited is very expensive. Volkswagen have never changed any model just for the sake of it and there was no point investing in a new model when this one was proving popular in European and American markets – buyers who wanted a small quality soft top would always opt for a Golf. They did not worry that it was the old shape, after all this was a design classic and the razor edged styling suited the convertible. Hence the decision to skip a generation and wait for the arrival of the A3 (Mark 3) body.

TRUE COLOURS

Although the Mark 1 body style was a constant, the variable factor was the name of the model, which veered from convertible to cabriolet. The special editions monopolized the cabriolet name. Initially there were all black, followed by all white special editions. The latter proved incredibly popular and by 1986 it accounted for almost a third of sales in the UK.

The 'All White' came with full colour keyed bodywork including the spoiler, bumpers and door mirrors. The white theme continued on the upholstery, with a white hood, seat cloth (offset with some black horizontal stripes) and leatherette

Strange but true. In 1983 Volkswagen's Development put a Karmann to sea, to see how an engine behaved when used for water propulsion. This was no ordinary engine, being supercharged to produce anything between 150 and 170bhp. A modified differential allowed it to drive a four bladed propeller at the rear.

143

Here is the missing link between the A1 and A3 (Mark 1 and Mark 3) versions of the Golf convertible. Several firms in Europe lifted the lid on the Mark 2 Golf, but few did it as neatly as this example by Kamei. No roll bar, no bulging hood, but what now looks like a very dated body kit.

bolsters. Only the 5.5J × 13in alloy wheels remained silver, an oversight corrected by the CC, which had these letters embossed on the blue hood. The interior was also blue from the seat trim to the carpets. Volkswagen took the highly popular mix and match colour scheme theme and in 1987 turned it into the Quartet range available on the now officially designated 1.6 Cabriolet and 1.8 GTI Convertible. There were four exterior colours on offer – Alpine White, Paprika Red, Helios Blue and Sapphire Grey – with colour keyed bumpers, wheel arches and door mirrors, along with four upholstery options and four hood finishes. There were 64 permutations in all!

By 1989 the Quartet colour options doubled to eight exterior colours, with three hood colours and a new range of upholstery trim, which included part leather seats. These Quartets were re-badged simply as GTIs and remained an option on the Clipper. However, Volkswagen had not yet finished playing the special edition game.

In 1991 at the suggestion of the UK importers, the design department came up with an overtly sporting convertible. The Sportline had Recaro sports seats in black and red trim, red needled instruments 6J × 15in alloy wheels and either red or black paintwork combined with a black hood. If buyers did not fancy black or red, then the contemporary Rivage model offered Classic Blue metallic paintwork, Mauritius Blue cloth and an Indigo Blue hood. To top them all, the Golf GTI Rivage Leather had beige leather interior, seats, door handles, hand brake grip and gear lever gaiter, with the alternative choice of Classic Green Pearl metallic paint and a black hood.

THIRD TIME LUCKY

When it came to making the new generation A3 (Mark 3) bodies go topless, Volkswagen turned to the company it knew best, Karmann. Who better to open up a Golf? As usual there were massive

144

Apart from the Clipper, which soldiered on to 1993, the last of the old shape convertibles imported to the UK were special edition GTI Sportline and Rivage models. Pictured here is the Rivage trimmed in leather with electric windows and alloy wheels as standard.

reinforcements in the floor, beneath the dashboard and at the front and rear ends. In torsional stiffness and solidity it was again a class leader.

An innovation was a the use of vibration dampers to counteract the scuttle shake that afflicts most convertibles. The first damper consisted of a precision calculated additional weight at the rear of the car. The second weighed in at 440lb (200kg) and was located at the front. It was attached to the engine/transmission block, which had mountings specially modified for the convertible (the manual gearbox version had five mountings, the automatic four). The dampers were an elastically suspended mass. When the body shell moved, this mass initially remained motionless due to

A pre-production prototype passes the roll test with flying colours. That roll bar makes all the difference.

its inertia but the motion of the body shell was eventually transmitted to it via the elastic mounting. If the body shell motion was reversed, the inertia of the damper meant that it initially continued in the same direction as before. As a result, the damper mass vibrated in phase opposition to the body shell and the unwanted vibrations were suppressed. The new convertible did not wobble like a jelly.

AVANTGARDE, GREEN AND PINK

The new model was badged as a Cabriolet and launched in the UK with a choice of just two models. The entry level 1.8 came with the standard 90bhp engine. Apart

from that cosy, six layer, insulated hood, the specification matched the hatchbacks for safety equipment – including side impact beams – and came with driver and passenger air bags. Sports seats, electric windows, colour keyed bumpers and mirrors, and a folding rear seat were all part of the package. For sportier drivers the 2.0 Cabriolet Avantgarde offered the GTI's 115bhp unit and plenty of standard equipment. Alloy wheels and sports suspension gave the Avantgarde a distinctly GTI flavour, and the power hood made life very much easier.

In 1995 Volkswagen introduced a new convertible concept and proved that soft tops were not just fun, but frugal too. (Frugal certainly, but was it the right stylish image? What the world got was the first

After releasing the catches on the windscreen, all it takes is the press of a button to lower and fold away the hood.

A 2.0 Avantgarde on the beach. It is the closest thing to an open topped GTI with the new Karmann converted A3 (Mark 3) body.

Golf Avantgarde

Engine

Design	Four cylinder in line, toothed belt driven SOHC
Materials	Alloy cylinder head, cast iron block transversely mounted in front
	Digifant fuel injection
	Catalytic converter
	Lambda control
Capacity	1,984cc
Bore	82.5 × 92.8mm
Output	115bhp at 5400rpm
Compression ratio	10.4:1
Maximum torque	166Nm at 3200rpm

Transmission

	Front wheel drive
5-speed	3.45, 1.94, 1.29, 0.97, 0.81:1
Reverse	3.17:1
Final drive	3.67:1

Suspension

Front	Coil springs and shock absorbers, suspension strut and lower wish bone, track stabilizing steering roll radius
Rear	Torsion beam axle, anti-roll bar

Steering

Power steering, rack and pinion

Brakes

Dual circuit servo
Asbestos free linings
Ventilated front discs, solid rear

Tyres and wheels

185/60VR-14H on 6J × 14in alloys

Dimensions

Track – front	57.6in (1,464mm)
Track – rear	56.2in (1,428mm)
Wheelbase	97.4in (2,475mm)
Length	158.3in (4,020mm)
Width	66.7in (1,695mm)
Height	55.1in (1,400mm)
Unladen weight	2,819lb (1,280kg)

Performance

Top speed	118mph (190kph)
Acceleration	0–60mph in 11.2 seconds

Fuel consumption

33.8mpg (8.3 litres per 100km)

diesel powered convertible.) The TDI Cabriolet had the 90hp 1.9 litre unit, which provided brisk rather than stunning performance, reaching 60mph in 13 seconds and giving a top speed of 107mph (172kph). Of course 54mpg (5.2 litres per 100km) was the pay back, as was open air motoring. Unfortunately, even though this diesel was quiet it still made the unmistakable clattering noise, especially at idle.

To coincide with their sponsorship of the 1994 European tour by the rock band Pink Floyd, Volkswagen released a very special psychedelic edition. It was finished exclu-

sively in Sound Blue metallic paint and had Pink Floyd graphics on the bodywork and interior trim. The specification of the 2.0 litre model was comprehensive and included a power operated hood, central locking, electric windows, sports seats, a Sony CD player and alloy wheels. Just 30 lucky owners got to take a trip in one.

Karmann's convertibles were always beautifully built, strong and stylish. The first Golf convertible was a true classic that broke the tired old sports car mould and launched a raft of imitators that fell far short of the original. The later model was

Fresh air and diesel fumes do go together with the unique Golf TDI cabriolet. Clean emissions and an open top roof see to that.

plump and less assured, but only because the Mark 3 on which it was based was not as inspiring as it ought to have been. However, Karmann regularly come up with exciting prototypes and proposals, so maybe something unconventional will be given the go-ahead in the near future. So long as there is a Volkswagen that needs the open air treatment, it seems that there will always be a Karmann convertible.

On stage, the very limited edition Pink Floyd cabriolet.

The Kleinwagen GL, a 1985 proposal by Karmann based on the running gear of a Golf. The idea was to build a low cost convertible that would appeal to young buyers. Construction was to be from composite material. The strength of the structure resulted from all the roof pillars and rails remaining in place. This meant that the roof could be removed, allowing a simple hood to be rolled back like an alternative soft top Targa. An intriguing concept that should have been given a chance.

Coupe's

KARMANN

Cabriolets

©1996 JAMES RUPERT

SCIROCCO (1974-81) KARMANN BUILT AND GIUGIARO STYLED VARIATION ON THE GOLF THEME. MUCH BETTER THAN THE OLD KARMANN GHIA AND THE GTI ENGINED GLi BEST OF ALL

CABRIOLET (1980-93) VW INVENTED THE 'HOT HATCH' AND KARMANN BROUGHT BACK THE CABRIOLET. THEY EVEN COMBINED THE TWO WITH THE GLi AND GTi VERSIONS.

SCIROCCO 2 (1982-92) KARMANN BUILT OF COURSE, BUT VW STYLED, SOFTER SHAPE AND HANDLING THE RESULT. HOWEVER, SHORT LIVED 16V REDRESSED THE PERFORMANCE BALANCE.

CABRIOLET (1988-93) IT IS STILL A MARK 1 GOLF UNDERNEATH, BUT A MID LIFE RESTYLE RESULTED IN A SOFTER BUMPERS AND SIDE SKIRTS, PLUS COLOUR KEYING.

CORRADO (1989-95) BASED ON THE GOLF BUT NOT A SCIROCCO REPLACEMENT. 136 BHP 16V, OR SUPERCHARGED 160 BHP G60. 1992 2.8 190 BHP VR6 FASTEST EVER VOLKSWAGEN

CABRIOLET 3 (1993-?) AFTER MISSING OUT ON THE MARK 2, KARMANN BROUGHT BACK THE CABRIOLET IN A BIGGER, SAFER AND GREENER GOLF 3. DIESEL MODEL IS A WORLD FIRST.

151

10 Golf Gets the Boot – Jetta and Vento

'The most successful skin graft in modern automotive history' – Peter Vack, *Volkswagen Buyer's Guide.*

In the summer of 1979 Volkswagen gave the Golf a boot and called it the Jetta. Coming up with a three box saloon had been a bit of an afterthought. The versatility and practicality of the hatchback concept – not pioneered by Volkswagen, but exploited to brilliant effect by the Golf – did not apparently suit all tastes and many buyers appreciated the more conventional appeal of a saloon. Obviously the separate luggage compartment is a more secure place to store valuables. A saloon is also a much larger and imposing vehicle where business credibility rather than load carrying practicality is

Anyone with a set of suitcases like these could always rely on a Jetta's boot to swallow them up.

A Jetta cutaway, showing that huge boot to excellent effect.

more important. As a result the Jetta has always been perceived as the rather dull relative of the otherwise stylish and ground breaking Golf. In almost every market except America the Jetta struggled while the Golf flourished. However, it always stacked up rather well against the Golf when it came to performance and practicality.

DULL BUT ROOMY JETTA

What made the Jetta different from the Golf was an extra 155.1in (3,800mm) in length. Although the wheelbase was exactly the same the extra body length contained an absolutely huge boot. It added up to 22.2cu ft (630 litres) of luggage space, a 70 per cent improvement over the Golf. Not surprisingly, the weight went up by more than 110lb (50kg), but this did not seem to affect the performance, which remained similar to the Golf thanks to decent aero-

dynamics. The other way that you could tell which car was a Jetta was the re-styled front end, distinguished by rectangular headlamps, integral lip spoiler and fancy wheel trims.

UK drivers did not get to grips with the Jetta's many benefits until March 1980 and even then the UK market only got the option of the four door body. The first line-up comprised 1.3 L and GL models, a 1.5 LS and GLS and a 1.6 GLi. In September 1980, in line with the Golf, the interior was tidied up, but a year later there was a wholesale revision of the range. In came the 1.1 C Formel E, which like the Golf offered increased economy. The L became a C, the 1.3 GL was discontinued, the LS mutated into the CL, 1.5 GLS became the GL and in came a 1.6 C diesel. The specification changes were minor, simply interior trim upgrades and black bumpers.

The last variant was the LX saloon in September 1983. Based on the 1.3 C, which benefited from some bright work around

Rarely seen in the UK, a 2-door Jetta, here in exciting turbo diesel trim.

A GLi hurries to an appointment with a packed boot no doubt.

the bumper and window surrounds, it had 5.5 J steel wheels topped off with chrome wheel trims and a sliding steel sunroof. Inside, it had a centre console and black or brown tweed cloth.

Rather than being an alternative to the Golf, the Jetta succeeded in making rival saloons look less well booted and poorly built – even if it could be described as a trifle dull. The trouble with the Jetta is that it was always regarded as an afterthought. Maybe the new model would put matters and buyers' perceptions right.

NEW JETTA

The Jetta was intended to be part of the overall Mark 2 range right from the launch. Once again, the wheelbase was the same, but attaching that huge 23cu ft (652 litres) of boot on the back of the Jetta meant at 176.1in (4,315mm) it was some 13.4in (330mm) longer than the Golf. Like the Golf there was a big improvement in rear seat passenger space and the drag coefficient was a respectable 0.36. Like the old Jetta the new one was distinguishable from the hatched Golf not only by the huge boot, but the distinctive rectangular headlamps. Nevertheless, it failed to set the pulse racing.

The new Jetta was launched in September 1984, some seven months after the Golf, and comprised five models, although the CLD diesel made a mid summer appearance in July 1984. On the petrol front the base C was powered by the 1.3, a

Bigger, better and even more booted, a Mark 2 Jetta in GL trim skates on thin ice.

CL Formel E featured the same power unit plus economy gearbox, and the bigger engined models were the 1.6 GL and a 1.8 GLX. There was a comprehensive overhaul of the range during 1985 as the Formel, CL, GLX and CLD models were dropped. The CL Turbo diesel was finally upgraded to match the oil burning Golf model. In September the 1.3 C got hydraulic tappets and the 4+E gearbox. A new TX was introduced and the GL was upgraded to 1.8 power. Most significantly, the Jetta became almost exciting as the GT model received the Golf GTI's fuel injected 112bhp engine.

The next big leap forward for the Jetta was in 1987, when the wholesale improvements that made the Golf more UK and driver friendly – nearside parking wipers, deletion of front quarterlights and interior facelifts – were applied to the saloon. By far the most exciting development, however, was the GTI 16-valve: a real wolf in rather sheepish saloon bodywork. The ride height was lowered by 0.4in (10mm) and the 6J × 14in sports wheels were shod with 185/60 tyres. The 8-valve GT also gained in credibility when it was re-badged as a GTI.

From August 1989 there was an out-

Not all Jettas are booted and boring. Long before the Vento VR6 this Integrated Research Volkswagen in 1985 combined a whole range of experimental features destined to enter production. Power was provided by a supercharged version of the 1.8 engine, which produced 180bhp and translated into 130mph (209kph) top speed and 7 seconds to 60mph. The other innovations included air suspension, ABS brakes, ASR anti-slip control and an on-board navigation computer.

A Synchro version was always part of the European Jetta line-up. This is an improved 1987 model with a three bar grille, chrome badges, italic badge script and most important of all, no front quarterlight.

Jetta GTI 16-valve
Engine

Four cylinder in line, toothed belt driven SOHC
Alloy cylinder head, cast iron block transversely mounted in front
Bosch K-Jetronic fuel injection

Capacity	1,781cc
Bore	81 × 86.4mm
Output	139bhp at 6100rpm
Compression ratio	10.0:1
Maximum torque	133lb/ft at 4600rpm

Transmission

Front wheel drive

5-speed	3.46, 2.12, 1.44, 1.13, 0.91:1
Reverse	3.17:1
Final drive	3.67:1

Suspension

Lower ride height

Front	Independent with MacPherson struts, lower wishbones, uprated coil springs and anti-roll bar
Rear	Semi-independent with trailing arms, torsion beam, uprated coil springs (20 per cent stiffer), telescopic dampers and anti-roll bar

Steering

Rack and pinion
3.7 turns lock to lock (power option 3.2)

Brakes

Larger pistons, 10.1in ventilated front discs, 8.9in (226mm) solid rear discs
Vacuum servo

Tyres and wheels

185/60VR-13 on 6J × 14in alloys
1989	185/55VR-15 on 6J

Dimensions

Track – front	56in (1,422mm)
Track – rear	56in (1,422mm)
Wheelbase	97in (2,464mm)
Length	172.8in (4,390mm)
Width	66.1in (1,680mm)
Height	55.5in (1,410mm)
Unladen weight	2,224lb (1,010kg)

Performance

Top speed	127mph (204kph)
Acceleration	0–60mph in 8.3 seconds

Fuel consumption

33.8mpg (8.3 litres per 100km)

Jetta Synchro

Engine

                Four cylinder in line, toothed belt driven SOHC
                Alloy cylinder head, cast iron block transversely mounted in front
                Bosch K-Jetronic fuel injection

Capacity	1,781cc
Bore	81 × 86.4mm
Output	90bhp at 5250rpm
Compression ratio	9.0:1
Maximum torque	142Nm at 3000rpm

Transmission

                Front wheel drive
                5-speed

Suspension

Front	Independent with MacPherson struts, lower wishbones, coil springs and anti-roll bar
Rear	Semi-independent with trailing arms, torsion beam, coil springs, telescopic dampers and anti-roll bar

Steering

                Rack and pinion
                3.7 turns lock to lock (power option 3.2)

Brakes

                Ventilated front discs, 8.9in (226mm) solid rear discs
                Vacuum servo

Tyres and wheels

                185/60VR-13 on 6J × 14

Dimensions

Track – front	56in (1,422mm)
Track – rear	56in (1,422mm)
Wheelbase	97in (2,464mm)
Length	172.8in (4,390mm)
Width	66.1in (1,680mm)
Height	55.5in (1,410mm)
Unladen weight	2,423lb (1,100kg)

Performance

Top speed	107mph (172kph)
Acceleration	0–62mph 12.1 seconds

Fuel consumption

Overall	25.9mpg (10.9 litres per 100km)

break of colour coding on the bumpers, a deeper front spoiler and black mouldings around the wheel arches and on the sills. The final design fling occurred in November 1990 when deeper and smoother bumpers were fitted across the range, which now comprised 1.3 LX, a catalysed 1.6 TX and GX, 1.8 GL, GTI and GTI 16v, diesel GX and turbocharged GLT. Although the 1.8 GX soldiered on until November 1992, the Jetta effectively died in October 1991. It was replaced by the Vento a year later.

VENTO – A BREATH OF FRESH AIR?

Just as the Jetta was essentially a Golf with a boot, so the Vento was a Mark 3 with an even bigger boot. (Vento is Italian and Portuguese for wind. Apparently more than 3,000 names were suggested and they had to pick this one – to suggest freshness and mobility.) The luggage capacity was 19.4cu ft (550 litres) with a European specification space saver tyre. The lid conveniently extended down to the bumper, with double jointed hinges mounted on the outer edges

The far from sluggish 16-valve Jetta, badged as a GTX in Germany and a GTI in the UK.

of the compartment to prevent luggage from being damaged. For hatchback-like versatility the rear seat had a split-folding back-rest. Volkswagen claimed that it was the first car in its class to have a lockable back-rest to prevent unlawful entry from the boot.

Volkswagen pitched the model as the missing link between the Golf and the Passat. Certainly from the 1996 model year, when the grille surround was given a facelift, it is hard to tell the difference between the dull but worthy Passat and the equally dull but slightly smaller Vento. Whatever Volkswagen said about the Vento, pitching it in the medium car sector away from the Golf and head to head with the Cavalier and Sierra hatchbacks was

not wholly convincing.

The range on the Continent was larger and slightly more interesting than in the UK. A GT model came with a choice of engines – either a standard 90bhp 1.8, or a hot 2.0 with the Golf GTI 115bhp unit, 'Plus' suspension 6.5x15 alloy wheels and a rear spoiler. There was a 1.9, 75bhp diesel option badged as the GTD. In the UK the 2.0 model was identified as a dowdy GL.

The most remarkable Vento of all was the VR6. Like the Golf version it came with 'Plus' running gear: optimized axle kine-matics, gas filled shock absorbers at the rear and electronic differential lock. It should have been regarded as a competi-tion for the Mercedes 190, but the curse of the booted Golf followed it to the showroom

The Vento seen from its best angle. This is the smooth and powerful VR6.

as buyers regarded it as little more than a reliable Volkswagen with two more cylinders. An unassuming model in all outward appearances, it actually had more feel and handling balance than the hatchback.

Unfortunately the Vento never had or will have – even in VR6 form – any of the Golf's charisma. That will be the perennial problem for any booted version of the Golf, whatever windy name it happens to be called.

A VR6 on the move.

Vento VR6

Engine

	15-degree V6 cylinder SOHC
	Alloy cylinder head, cast iron block transversely mounted in front
	Bosch Motronic fuel injection
Capacity	2,792cc
Bore	81 × 90.3mm
Output	174bhp at 5000rpm
Compression ratio	10.0:1
Maximum torque	235Nm at 4200rpm

Transmission

	Front wheel drive
5-speed	3.30, 1.94, 1.31, 1.03, 0.84:1
Reverse	3.06:1
Final drive	3.68:1

Suspension

Front	MacPherson struts with lower wishbones, 0.4in (10mm) lower height, anti-roll bar, track stabilizing steering geometry

Rear	Torsion beam axle with track-correcting bearings anti-roll bar, uprated 'Plus' specification

Steering

	Power steering, rack and pinion 0.8in (20mm) lower

Brakes

	Dual circuit, servo, asbestos free linings Ventilated front discs, solid rear

Tyres and wheels

	205/50VR-15V on 6.5J × 15in alloys

Dimensions

Track – front	57.6in (1,464mm)
Track – rear	57in (1,448mm)
Wheelbase	97.4in (2,475mm)
Length	172.4in (4,380mm)
Width	66.7in (1,695mm)
Height	56.1in (1,425mm)
Unladen weight	2,665lb (1,210kg)

Performance

Top speed	140mph (225kph)
Acceleration	0–60mph in 7.8 seconds

Fuel consumption

	28.8mpg (9.8 litres per 100km)

From the front this 1996 specification Vento looks almost identical to the Passat. A victim of the same charisma bypass-operation?

11 Rabbit, Rabbit, Rabbit

'A Bullfrog that has swallowed a cardboard box' – Bill Mitchell of General Motors on the Volkswagen Rabbit.

America loved the reliable and quirky Beetle, despite its lack of practicality and speed. It may have been the first 'world car', popular in many markets and assembled on several continents, but there was room for something much more modern, and the Golf turned out to be the right car at the right time. In a depressed post fuel crisis market, its economy was welcome. The hatchback concept was not unique, but it had never been this well executed. Not only that, it was fun to drive. So in the gargantuan, gas guzzling American car market such a perfectly packaged sub compact should have been a sensation. But the bucked toothed Rabbit had a few teething troubles. First of all, where on earth did they get that name from?

You might have thought that the Golf would have been the perfect name for a new small car in America, where many people are obsessed by knocking little white balls into holes. However, after the success of the Beetle, and that was nicknamed after an insect, surely an association with a cuddly furry animal would boost popularity? So Rabbit the Golf became. There have been suggestions that the name indicated that the car was compact and fast, with sharp handling.

America's love affair with Volkswagen began with the Beetle. It is January 1949 and here Dutchman Ben Pon ships the first example. By the end of the year just two had been sold.

163

For no logical reason the Golf was re-badged as a Rabbit in America with a cuddly 'run rabbit' logo.

The long-term plan was to build Golfs on the American continent, but phase one involved exporting direct from Wolfsburg. Apart from being re-christened Rabbit, these 3- and 5-door sedans were between 100 and 200lb (45 and 90kg) heavier than European specification Golfs, because of the requirement to comply with emission and safety legislation. Not surprisingly, that made them fairly sluggish. The original 1,471cc engine was fed by Bosch K-Jetronic fuel injection, which produced 71bhp at 5,800rpm. Just about everything on the specification list was optional, from a 3-speed automatic gearbox to radial tyres. 'Poverty specification' was no ironic description – all buyers got on the entry level model was a single instrument dial and rubber mats.

The cost was $3,000, just $100 more expensive than the Super Beetle, which had been so popular. However, Deluxe and Performance options were available to make the Rabbit just that bit more friendly. They certainly did not come much more frugal than the 52mpg (5.4 litres per 100km) highway and 37mpg (7.6 litres per 100km) town figures achieved by the diesel models. Not surprisingly, diesels accounted for almost 50 per cent of Rabbit sales in the first few years.

LAME RABBITS

The Rabbit also made friends with the *Road and Track* testers when it was launched. They liked the design, handling and performance. Unfortunately, the initial batch of imports during 1975 and 1976 had plenty of problems to upset the American buyer. Build quality was way below par and there were an unacceptable number of squeaks and rattles on the inside from poorly fitted

The first Westmoreland built Rabbit for the USA – the date is 1978.

trim. But that was the least of Volkswagen's problems. Mechanically there were lots of minor problems with the exhaust, brakes and cooling system. Then some engines started to fail; diesels in particular were badly affected by oil leaks, snapping crankshafts, splitting cylinder heads and sick fuel filters. Oil pressure could sometimes rise alarmingly and blow the oil filters right off the block. Apparently the number one repair for petrol engined Rabbits in the first two years was the complete replacement of the engine; Volkswagen's warranty claims must have been horrendous. Even so, *Road and Track* still seriously rated the diesel engine in particular after theirs had covered over 100,000 miles (160,000km). It too needed a rebuild, but they still calculated running costs at just 11 cents per mile (7 cents per km).

In 1976 something was done about the lack of power as the 1,588cc reached dizzy 90bhp heights. But 1979 saw a change to a short stroke 1,457cc unit pumping out a measly 72bhp, which was later again downgraded to 63bhp. In the meantime Volkswagen of America had got their factory in Westmoreland County, Pennsylvania on stream in 1978. It produced a 1,716cc engine that proved to have more torque and a respectable 75bhp output. Two new models perked up the Rabbit range for 1980 as the 1,588cc unit became standard.

The convertible and pick-up were significant and popular variants. The pick-up, built at Westmoreland, had a longer wheelbase – 103.3in (2,624mm) compared to the Rabbit's 94.5in (2,400mm) – and was an instant hit because of the front wheel drive configuration that left a long flat rear load bay. In the American market it was a small and practical alternative to the giant native examples offered at the time. Production ceased in 1983.

183-ZGY
113-EWJ
spect that, with the
down, a Rabbit has more cargo area
leetwood."
ket for a small second car. When he showed me
t had, I ended up with a big first car: Rabbit."
tually three feet shorter than some mid-sized cars. Which
eeze into parking spaces other drivers have to pass up.
his has led some skeptics to believe you can't squeeze a lot
, flip open our hatchback, and the Rabbit gives you 11.3
to. If you can temporarily afford to do without a back seat,
you a carpeted compartment that's larger than a Cadillac
need all this room, simply flip the back seat up. A carpeted
store valuables out of view."
ve got to load up to
eve this cargo area.

Early Rabbit advertising emphasized the deceptively large 'cargo area' compared to America's own models.

Rectangular headlights, as well as those big ugly bumpers meant that it was impossible to mistake a Westmoreland-built Rabbit for an import. This is a 1981 S, which at the time was the hottest Rabbit allowed out of captivity in the American market. It had a standard-tune engine, but GTI suspension and interior.

TOPLESS RABBITS

Karmann's convertible was never built in America, but it proved to be very big hit, registering sales in excess of 100,000 by 1990. Roomy, reliable and relatively cheap it took over from where the ever popular Beetle cabriolet and Karmann Ghia left off. Introduced with the 1,588cc engine, catalytic converter and lowered compression ratio of 8.2:1 it came with European GTI suspension. The body style barely changed over the years, with just minor facelifts in line with European versions. Dual headlamps in 1989 brought the model visually into line with the rest of the world and the Cabriolet Classic special edition in 1993 celebrated thirty seven years of Volkswagen convertibles. This model was almost identical to the UK edition Rivage. Most models since the mid 1980s have been finished in GTI trim with a 1,780cc 90bhp unit rising to 94bhp in 1993.

America did not have to wait long for the Mark 3 convertible. In 1994 it came with the 2.0 litre 115bhp engine and by 1996 it had dual airbags and ABS brakes as standard. It was badged as a Cabriolet.

FLASH RABBITS

By the early 1980s the Rabbit was under the weather in the States and in need of

Big in America, more than 100,000 Karmann convertibles were sold. This is a 1983 Wolfsburg edition with white alloy wheels, hood, upholstery and door trim. Yummy.

some veterinary attention. The Golf had been so compromised for the American market that there was little of its original character left. Not only were the speed and handling a big disappointment – thanks to all the safety and emissions gear – but it looked bad. In an effort to adapt the specification to the American market there were unwise cosmetic additions to the interior and exterior. Bad upholstery fabrics, garish exterior colours and decals hardly helped.

Furthermore, the Rabbits were not screwed together very well. Anyone used to Beetle build quality was very unpleasantly surprised by the less than perfect Rabbit. To make matters worse the Rabbit was under attack from the increasingly competent Japanese imports and a strengthening Deutschmark, which pushed up prices – $6,920 was a lot to pay in 1981 for the com-

mon or garden Rabbit. Worst of all, the Americans were denied the most exciting version, the GTI.

America had to wait a very long time for the GTI. Journalists had known about this potent little motor for many years and in November 1981 the *Motor Trend* staff went as far as penning an open letter to Volkswagen of America to state their case for allowing it into the country. They reckoned that it would not cost much to introduce, could be competitively priced and 'give Americans a reason to leave their Porsches at home'. While a nation waited they were placated with the decidedly tame Rabbit S, which had GTI suspension and interior, but a standard-tune 1,716cc engine.

The journalists' prayers were answered just a year after that letter. In 1982 the GTI arrived, but it had been a close thing. According to Volkswagen of America the original plan had simply been the installation of sports seats and beefier GTI suspension to the existing Rabbit S. Luckily the decision was made to use the new 1,781cc engine. The result was a lower compression ratio (9.5:1) than the European model (10:1) and it produced 91bhp. It had a GTI gearbox, but a higher (3.94:1) final drive ratio. Because it carried so much more weight than a European GTI, including air conditioning in the hotter states, the suspension was beefed up. The spring rates were therefore 22 per cent stiffer at the front and 29 per cent at the rear, and the rear dampers were also uprated. It had the wider 6J × 14in alloy wheels from the Passat, fitted with Pirelli P6 tyres. The car looked slightly different from European models, because apart from the bigger wheels and impact bumpers, there was a distinctively different grille with rectangular headlamps. The driver sat on corduroy seats instead of cloth and

The GTI was long overdue, but finally arrived to complete the Rabbit line-up. These are 1984 cars – a GTI up front, an L behind and a GL bringing up the rear.

looked at a shiny brushed aluminium finish around the fascia. The car was badged as the Volkswagen GTI.

Gaining the GTI badge was good news – all of a sudden drivers were taking the car seriously. At last there was some decent performance to shout about and along with that came European levels of refinement. By then the GTI was an old car, but it rapidly won new friends. Volkswagen of America predicted a modest sales target of 12,000 for the first year, but they sold 27,782. *Car and Driver* called it 'the car we have all been waiting for'. They also reckoned that it 'works so well, you would swear it came from Wolfsburg'.

Despite that commendation, Westmoreland closed in 1988. Building cars in high-cost America did not make financial sense as the 1980s progressed. The rising popularity of Japanese compact cars and a levelling off in car sales meant that the plant could not be justified, so Golfs were obtained from the Volkswagen assembly plant in Mexico.

GOLF POPS OUT OF THE HAT

Before Golf sales went into the doldrums, the Mark 2 model was introduced in 1984 and proved to be just as popular. The Rabbit name was killed off; from now on it was called the Golf (except for the GTI, which remained the Volkswagen GTI). The new range was straightforward enough, based around the 1.7 and 1.8 engines. *Road Track* thought that the Golf 'was bigger and better than the Rabbit' and added 'the GTI has no flaws'. Even so, the GTI was pepped up in 1987 when the 16-valve head replaced the 8-valve to produce 123bhp at 5,800rpm, significantly improving low speed torque. This coincided with the introduction of a 102bhp Golf GT.

A full 2.0 litre GTi arrived in 1990 – a Passat 1,984cc engine was installed and topped off with the 16-valve head, boosting output to 134bhp with significantly more torque. Even the 8-valve engine used in the Golf and Jetta GL was improved too so that the output remained the same at 105bhp, but there were considerable improvements

The GTI was never badged as a Golf, but as a Volkswagen GTI.

GTI Mark 3 American style, a standard 2.0 litre car with cosmetic GTI additons and a manual gearbox. However, they did not have to wait long for the VR6 GTI.

in torque. However, these developments were not enough to halt sliding sales of no more than a few thousand GTIs annually.

Two years after the European launch, the Golf Mark 3 (Golf III in America) arrived in March 1993 in 3-door, 5-door and cabriolet versions. The standard engine was the new 2.0 litre, 115bhp unit. The GTI was available simply as a manual transmission alternative and badged as a 'Sport'. It had no more power – just revised trim, alloy wheels and a GTI badge.

In 1994 Volkswagen America installed the rather more powerful 172bhp VR6 engine to create the Volkswagen GTI VR6. For the 1996 model year the Roman numeral III was dropped from the Golf designation. The Sport was renamed 'GTI' and came with dual airbags and a glove box. A

new power plant also joined the line-up, the European direct injection turbocharged diesel.

GOLF IN CANADA

Canadians had cause for celebration in 1978 as the first country on the American continent to get hold of the GTI. Identical to the European car, its only outward differences were 5mph (8kph) impact bumpers and narrow 5in rims.

GOLF IN SOUTH AFRICA

This has always been a fascinating market and the company there is a wholly owned

Unique to the South African market, an entry-level Chico Citi.

subsidiary of Volkswagen. In performance terms, they produced their own versions of the GTI, first with a 86bhp version of the 1.6 engine and badged a GTS. Then in 1983 they launched their own GTi. The specification was always high and the suspension was tuned for local conditions. Most interesting of all is the fact you can still buy all three series of Golfs, from the entry level Chico Citi, which is as Giugiaro intended, through to the Mark 2 and Mark 3.

GOLF IN YUGOSLAVIA

In 1972 the state run Yugoslavian importer UNIS formed a new company with Volkswagen called TAS (Tvornica Automobila Sarajevo) to assemble Volkswagens. Although they produced Golfs, a unique model made it to western European markets in the shape of the Caddy pick-up. Available from 1982, it was based on the American pick-up built in Westmoreland between 1980 and 1983.

GOLF WORLDWIDE

At the time of writing 3,740 Golfs are built every day. Broken down by country the figures look like this:

Belgium	850
Germany	2,290 (Mosel 440, Osnabrück 180, Wolfsburg 1,670)
Mexico	410
Slovakia	50
South Africa	140

SCIROCCO USA

Rather alarmingly, the Scirocco was scheduled to be re-badged as the Blizzard for the American market. Luckily that did not happen. A single model was offered with the 1,471cc engine and single Zenith carburettor. Like contemporary Rabbits, the early Sciroccos were afflicted with engine problems and rampant rust. For the 1976 season the engine was increased to 1,555cc

171

Yugoslavian-built Golf Caddys. A good pun and a useful vehicle too.

American Scirocco. This is a 1980 S with a larger front spoiler and side stripes, similar to the European Storm, but no leather and those awfully big bumpers.

and a single windscreen wiper was standard. Bosch fuel injection was available from 1977. The 1,588cc engine and 5-speed gearbox in 1979 made the car easier to drive, but did not help the declining performance. The Scirocco S in 1980· was the American version of the Storm, although the interior was cloth rather than leather.

The Scirocco II was launched a year after the European equivalent was unveiled at the 1981 Geneva Motor Show. It came with a new 1,715cc engine, although the 74hp output stayed the same. By 1983 the engine was upped to 1,780cc and 90hp and performance improved so that it would reach 60mph in 10.7 seconds, go on to a top speed of 110mph (177kph), yet still return a respectable 27mpg (10.4 litres per 100km). 'Wolfsburg' limited editions were launched to pep up its showroom prospects with Passat alloy wheels, rear spoiler and black B-pillars. Increasingly the competition from Japan in the shape of the Honda Prelude and Toyota Celica made marketing a $10,000 coupé very difficult.

The search for more power ended in 1986 when the 16-valve head was bolted to the 1.8 block. New Bosch KE fuel injection, knock and Lambda sensors, plus a catalytic converter made it comply with American legislation. The resulting 123hp power represented a 33hp increase over the old 8-valve. In addition, stiffer springs, a larger rear anti-roll bar, 185/60HR-14 tyres and rear discs made it a much more sporting package as the 7.7 seconds time to 60mph demonstrated. All of a sudden the Porsche 944 and Mazda RX7 were slower. Despite this and the fact that the slower 8-valve was discontinued in 1987, the Scirocco had to make way for a brand new coupé.

CORRADO USA

The supercharged Corrado G60 went to America in late 1989. Its 137mph (220kph) top speed and 0–60mph time of under 8 seconds impressed, as did the eminently reasonable $20,000 asking price. However, it was replaced in 1992 by the mildly improved VR6. In America it was prefixed by the letters SLC (Sports Luxury Coupé)

The re-styled Scirocco Mark 2 looked smoother, but got longer by a good 6.5in (165mm). Those mantelpiece bumpers probably had a lot to do with it. This is a 1982 model fitted with a 1.7 litre engine.

and like the Scirocco it trounced its rivals on performance and price.

JETTA USA

America could not always grasp the hatchback concept. It was something downmarket, small and cheap – and there were lots to choose from, the likely choice being something Japanese. So addition of a boot to the Rabbit in 1980 proved to be a master stroke. To American eyes it was not simply a Golf with an extremely large boot, but a luxurious European sedan. The standard velour trim was more luxurious than the Rabbit with the option of leatherette. Otherwise it was as the Rabbit when it came to suspension and 1.6 engine. Four doors were the norm, but a 2-door version was available as well as a wide range of model options, including a diesel and turbo diesel.

From 1981 the engine was upgraded to the more powerful 1,716cc unit. In 1984 the GLI made a big impact, being essentially a booted GTI, with the same engine, suspension and interior, although the extra 180lb

(82kg) of the boot made it a fraction slower than the hatchback. Anyone who loaded up the model with options like air conditioning could watch the retail price rise to a heady $10,000. This was almost in the BMW league, but the Jetta was not outclassed.

The car got better looking in 1985 when it was revised to become the Jetta II. Customers could choose between a 1.6, 52hp diesel, a 68hp turbocharged version, a 1,780cc, 85hp four cylinder, or a GLI version tuned to produce 100hp. The GLI got a major upgrade three years later as the 2.0 litre 16-valve engine was installed. Rapturous testers at *Road and Track* thought that this was a 'true sports sedan that likes to get physical'. They liked everything about the car from the handling to the 'anatomically correct leather wrapped steering wheel'.

The name Vento was not used in America, so the Jetta III arrived in 1993. It was re-styled and powered by the 2.0 litre unit used in the Golf. Volkswagen had a surprise for GLI devotees: out went the 16-valve head and in came the intoxicating 172hp VR6 engine from the Corrado. The

America loved the Jetta and this 1989 GLI had a 16-valve engine under the bonnet to make it even more desirable.

While Europe got the Vento, Americans know it as the Jetta III. This is s GL with the standard 2.0 litre engine.

all new GLX signalled that the Jetta was a major player and a real alternative to the compact six cylinder offerings from BMW and Mercedes. For 1996 the III designation was dropped so it became the Volkswagen

Jetta again. The specification now included dual airbags plus a glove box. There were GL, GLS and GLX models, the latter with a VR6 option.

12   The Golf Goes Racing

'The winningest Volkswagen ever' – Volkswagen America on the 16-valve.

Ferrari, Jaguar, Alfa Romeo – Volkswagen does not really trip off the tongue in the same way as those other legendary sporting names. Volkswagen was never a racing name to conjure with, until that is, the Golf came along.

The old Beetle had proved tough enough to survive the odd rally and was lots of fun in a one make race, but it was hard to take seriously. The Golf proved to be equally durable, occasionally anonymous, but largely Volkswagen's most successful competition car ever. The factory started preparing cars as early as 1974 when the motor sport department at Hanover put together a 1.5 litre Group 1 Golf for Formula 3 racer Freddy Kottulinsky. But it was the GTI that was to provide the real basis for sporting Golfs – the original production run was for 5,000 examples to meet the Group 1 Production Saloon regulations.

GOLF GOES RALLYING

The motor sport department at Volkswagen was run by Austrian Peter Rosorius who steered the Golf towards rallying. Engine preparation was down to local specialist firms and even on some occasions the Hanover University Science Department. The result was a 120bhp

based on the 1,598cc unit. The more flexible Group 2 class allowed for experimentation, so a revised cylinder head and Zenith fuel injection provided a welcome power boost to 180bhp. In the hands of Jochi Kleint, the tuned Golf got as high as second place in the 1978 Hunsruck Rally.

So the Golf proved to be truly competitive, especially when Swedish Rally legend Per Eklund drove a GTI to its first major victory in the 1979 Sachs–Baltic Rally. Eklund and the GTI beat 154 starters. The Swede continued the GTI association when in 1980 he contested the Monte Carlo Rally. He excelled in the particularly icy conditions and for much of the event kept the

This modified Group 2 Golf scored the model's first major victory in the 1979 Sachs–Baltic Rally.

GTI amongst the top three. Only when conditions improved did more powerful rivals catch up, forcing Eklund down to a still respectable fifth place. Like the Mini Cooper before it, the Golf may not have had immense power, but the superb handling, simplicity and toughness of the GTI meant that it could embarrass far more flamboyant machinery. It was no surprise when in 1981 GTIs dominated and won outright the German Rally Championship.

OETTINGER 16-VALVE

A new rally weapon was announced in 1981 to Group 4 specification: a 16-valve, twin overhead camshaft Oettinger cylinder that boosted the power further to 193bhp. With Eklund at the helm this car was entered in the 1982 San Remo Rally, a World Championship event, and held a top ten place before retirement due to clutch failure. Another Swede, Kalle Grundel, was drafted into the works driving seat after impressive performances in a privately entered GTI. He showed what he could do in the 1983 RAC Rally by finishing eighth overall and prompted Volkswagen to enter the World Rally Championships the following season.

In the world of rallying 1984 was a time

Alfons Stuck and Paul Schmuck were winners of the 1981 German Rally Championship, the Golf's first major championship win.

of change: the old classifications were scrapped and replaced by Group A for normal production based cars and Group B for purpose built specials like the Ford RS200. Not surprisingly the GTI, especially with a 1.8 power unit producing 160bhp seemed a natural for Group A. Its chances improved further with the arrival of the Mark 2 model midway through the season. Over 20 events the top finishes were at the Monte Carlo (9th), San Remo (6th) and Portuguese (8th).

It was decided to create a one-off World Championship title for Group A cars in the 1986 season. Swede Kenneth Eriksson was leading the chase for Volkswagen Motorsport and won three rallies outright that season: New Zealand, Argentina and San Remo. He had benefited from the installation of the new 16-valve engine since the 1000 Lakes event and by finishing second in the RAC Rally clinched the Golf's first world title.

The following season Volkswagen entered a two car team, the other being driven by German Erwin Webber. Eriksson again drove supremely well against tough, mainly Far East, opposition. The high-

Enter the Mark 2 GTI. Easier to drive and stronger, it was a consistent rather than outstanding performer, nevertheless Kenneth Eriksson and Peter Diekman won the 1986 Group A and 1987 two wheel drive World Rally Championships.

lights were second place in New Zealand, fourth in Argentina and outright victory in the Ivory Coast. At the end of the season Eriksson came in fourth overall and in the process won another one-off trophy in the shape of the Two Wheel Championship. The last international season for the GTI was 1989 and although off the pace most of the time, in the toughest event of all, the Safari Rally, former world champion Stig Blomqvist finished an impressive third after a particularly difficult event.

The car designed to take over from the GTI on the competition scene was the G60. Volkswagen even went so far as to say that the Rallye G60 had been 'designed to win the World Rallying Championship'. Unfortunately, production of the Rallye Golf at Volkswagen's Brussels plant was postponed and full motor sport homologation was delayed until 1990. The model's first event was the Acropolis Rally. It kept up with the leading pack but retired with a broken water pump belt. By the New Zealand event an overall third placing looked promising. However, a failure to finish the Australian event led to Volkswagen cancelling the works cars. The governing body prevented the supercharged car from running with unrestricted inlet dimensions to bring it in line with restricted turbocharged cars.

Although Volkswagen had severed official involvement with rallying they kept tabs on developments within the sport and went so far as to develop a feasibility study in 1992. This exercise involved designing a Golf that could win the 1994 World Rally Championship. The basis was a Mark 3 Golf with four wheel drive and a turbocharger. Schmidt Motorsport were asked to build a prototype, code named A59. At its heart was a radical all aluminium engine connected to a 6-speed gearbox that operated in conjunction with electronically con-

trolled centre and rear differentials. Although the design was approved and parts ordered by September 1992, financial gloom at Wolfsburg head office meant that the project was cancelled – though not before the world got a tantalising glimpse of what might have been when pictures of the concept were released.

Although the Mark 3 Golf continues to contest rally championships in the UK, Germany and Finland, official backing and the creation of a purpose-built Golf remain in doubt. In fact, it is surprising that the Golf has achieved so much success in view of Volkswagen's reluctance to stick with a racing programme for more than a few seasons. As a company they have never relied on competition success to sell their cars and see no reason to change that view. After all, the Beetle sold 20 million without a chequered flag in sight.

GTI IN BRITAIN

All it took was an advertisement for a silver left hand drive GTI, reputedly the first imported, to kick start the racing career of the Golf in the UK. The man who answered it and bought the car was Richard Lloyd. After unsuccessfully campaigning an Opel Commodore in 1976, Lloyd's performances the following season in a virtually standard car were enough to prompt Volkswagen GB to make an approach. With official backing Lloyd approached race preparation specialists Broadspeed. Their engine specialist Brian Ricketts was assigned to help. Both men soon appreciated that racing was an expensive business but believed that they could do a competitive job for Volkswagen or anyone else who wanted a Golf prepared for competition. The result was GTI Engineering, the legendary tuning company, and a string of class wins over the next

The Rallye Golf. From its name is should have been a contender, but it never was, despite capturing third place in the 1990 Rally of New Zealand with Erwin Weber at the wheel.

This is A59, the turbocharged, aluminium engined, four wheel drive Rally weapon that never got further than a full size concept.

Richard Lloyd's 1979 championship winning GTI in action and still competitive four years later in the hands of John Morris.

few seasons in saloon car championships.

Richard Lloyd is a significant figure and has inspired many drivers to take up racing in GTIs, which have come to dominate the national Slick 50 sponsored racing series. He also took the GTI into Europe, at the European Touring Car Championship race at Zolder. However, apart from other ETC wins and the Golf GTI Cup in Europe, which ran in Germany between 1977 and 1982, much of the serious circuit activity took place in the UK. Recently the Golf, in particular the Mark 1, has dominated domestic production saloon car series like the Slick 50 and 750 Motor Club Hot Hatch category.

In 1986 there was an interesting scheme to find a British rally star and the company invested £250,000 in the Volkswagen Junior Team. The selection process led to four drivers being taken on to drive GTIs. At the end of the season Simon Davison had taken the National Group A driver's title and for Volkswagen the National Rally Championship Manufacturer's Award. By 1989 Volkswagen had decided to simply run a bonus scheme for GTI competitors as the large numbers of Group N showroom

specification Golfs dominated rallying in the UK.

Volkswagen were officially back in rallying from 1994 when the Mark 3 Golf GTI 16-valve made its debut in the British Championship. They took advantage of the switch to the 'Formula 2' FIA rules (2 litres, two wheel drive). Taking 1994 as the learning year the Volkswagen team and rallying partner SBG Sport contested the British Rally Championship with drivers Dom Buckley and Tapio Laukkanen. The Finn competed in two rounds of the series and made a big impression with the bright yellow Sony sponsored 'Colour Concept' Golf in the RAC Rally and finished fourth in the F2 class.

The Volkswagen Vento VR6 Challenge was launched in 1994 as a successor to the Polo G40 Cup. Some racing glamour seems to have rubbed off on these competing Ventos, which have been regarded almost as a mini touring car series. These Ventos begin life as road going VR6s that were stripped to the shell and rebuilt with a safety cage and racing suspension, but with a standard VR6 engine supplied by Volkswagen and sealed by RAC inspectors

Paul Rose (73) ahead of Jonathan House. Rose won Class B in 1994 and was runner up in 95. He also prepares a number of cars in the series.

Roger Williams in a 16-valve car – used as his everyday transport during the week.

Dom Buckley and co-driver Nicky Beech competing in the 1995 British Rally Championship. Buckley helped develop the F2 Golf GTI during 1994. He gave the Golf its first rally victory in the 1995 Humberside Forest Rally.

Tapio Laukkanen's Colour Concept GTI, which finished fourth in the 1995 RAC Rally F2 class.

to prevent tampering. Modifications that are permitted under the regulations include fitting a dual throttle cable, any type of spark plug, plus Volkswagen Motorsport oil cooler and sump baffle. The suspension can be modified within certain parameters and Motorsport heavy duty anti-roll bars fitted; 7.5 × 16in Speedline wheels and Dunlop slicks and wet weather tyres are specified. Brakes are uprated, with huge ventilated discs at the front with AP Racing callipers, Mintex pads and

Tim Sugden lifts a wheel while taking part in the 1994 Scottish Mutual Volkswagen Vento VR6 Challenge.

Aeroquip brake hoses. The ABS system is removed.

GTI IN AMERICA

Just like every other place where Golfs are sent into racing combat, the model has proved to be the club competition stalwart in America. The simplicity and toughness of the Rabbit and Volkswagen GTI has made it a firm favourite over there. The model's finest year was 1987, when the GTI won no less than four national championships – the International Motor Sports Association Firestone Firehawk Touring Class; the Sports Car Club of America (SCCA) Escort Endurance Championship, Showroom Stock B Class; the SCCA PRO Rally Production Class; and the SCCA National Championship, Showroom Stock C.

As well as letting their warmed over GTIs do the talking in countless national and local competitions, Volkswagen were not averse to coming up with something special. To compete in one of America's most unusual annual events, Volkswagen put together one of the hottest and most bizarre Golfs ever. The event was the Pike's Peak Auto Hill Climb, the year was 1985 and the Golf had two Oettinger tuned 1.8 GTI engines. The result was 390bhp, a 0–60mph time of 4.6 seconds and a top speed of 162mph (261kph). In the red hot seat was 1979 European Rally Champion Jochi Klient. Unfortunately he was beaten by an Audi Quattro.

Undaunted, Volkswagen came back the following year, this time with a pair of 1.3 turbocharged Polo engines, one mounted at each end. Still no joy. Finally, in 1987 they bolted on two 16-valve turbocharged GTI

The ultimate competition Golf, with two Oettinger 16-valve engines on board giving a 160mph (257kph) top speed and a 0–62mph time of 4.6 seconds. Driven by Jochi Kleint, it failed to win the only race it was designed for, the Pike's Peak hill climb in Colorado.

units mounted longitudinally to accommo-date Hewland gearboxes and achieve 300bhp. Even with Klient in the driving seat they did not win, but this was a superb car.

FORMULA 3 GOLF GTI

It is possible to trace Volkswagen's involve-ment in serious competition back to 1965 and the importation from America of ten Beetle engined Formula Vee single seaters by Porsche. Its more powerful successor Super Vee proved to be an excellent train-ing ground for circuit racers such as 1982 World Champion Keke Rosberg, winner of the Super Vee title in 1975.

Development of the formula continued with the adoption of the water cooled Golf unit. This engine also leant itself to adap-tation for Formula 3, which used produc-tion based engines of up to 2 litres with a restricted air inlet that limited output to make racing closer and more competitive. Credit for the first conversion of a GTI goes to Siegfried Spiess in Stuttgart in 1978. Units tuned by John Judd appeared soon after and through the 1980s they dominat-ed Formula 3 in the UK and Germany. Significantly the series and engines gave breaks to such talents as Johnny Dumfries, Andy Wallace and Johnny Herbert.

13 Golfology

'The acquisition, refinement and enjoyment of the Volkswagen Golf' – *Concise Wolfsburg Dictionary*.

I hope that this book has tickled your Golf fancy. I should be very surprised if you have got this far into the book without feeling the urge to go out and buy one. After all, if you have not already bought a Golf, a Karmann convertible, Scirocco or Jetta, why not? If you already own a Golf, make it even more gorgeous with a body kit, or faster with some performance modifications. Maybe you own a Mark 3, but quite like the idea of running a Mark 1 for fun. Whatever you feel like doing, the Golf and its close relatives have much more potential than the average car. So let's start with the acquisition part of the Golfology equation.

BUYING BASICS

Before you take the used Volkswagen plunge sort out the financial side. Work out your buying budget and then stick to it. Get insurance quotes, especially for GTIs, Sciroccos and convertibles, as these cause the most problems when it comes to pumped up premiums. That annual figure alone could make your mind up for you as to whether you invest in a Volkswagen. It is always a good idea to leave a bit extra aside for parts, servicing and repairs.

When it comes to buying an older model that requires some work, remember that restorations will always cost double what you think they should. When you go shopping for cars try to take a dispassionate friend with you to discourage any irrational buys. Paying for a second opinion could save you making a big mistake, so an engineer's report is worth considering.

With all Volkswagens, a full service history is very reassuring as are lots of bills and a string of MOTs. Documentation is crucial and you should try to contact previous owners through the last registered keeper. Ask them about accidents and most important of all mileage. Volkswagens do not show their age and unscrupulous sellers will rewind the clock so that they can charge more.

Best of all, know your Volkswagen. Which model are you looking at? Is it the right specification? This book might help. The most important thing of all to remember is that if you have any doubts, just walk away – there are plenty more used Golfs to choose from.

GOLF MARK 1

That word 'classic' gets bandied about whenever the original model is mentioned, especially the GTI. It is often used to justify sky high prices, and certainly a good Mark 1 will be valued higher than a well used Mark 2. There is the added bonus that insurance companies might offer limited-use classic cover. But let us not get too carried away with the idea that every old GTI is a modern masterpiece. Not all Mark 1 Golfs are that good, or really worth having.

The first reason why they may not be tip top is that they have had much more time to disintegrate or be abused by an uncaring owner. Not only that, the early cars should really be the preserve of the die hard enthusiast. With a GTI, if your idea of fun is sitting on the wrong side of the cabin in a spartan little left hooker, then by all means track down one of the few specially imported cars. As for the old L model, if it has not already rusted into oblivion thanks to cheap Eastern Block steel, it is a dinosaur to drive. Go for a roomier Mark 2.

If you really do prefer the purity and uncluttered Giugiaro lines, linked to a punchy 1,800cc engine, with a good level of equipment that includes sunroof, alloy wheels and trip computer, then consider one of the 1983 GTI Campaign models. They had just about all the advantages of the forthcoming Mark 2 wrapped up in a pretty and lighter body. The dates to bear in mind are 1979 for the 5-speed gearbox option (standard from 1981) and 1983 for the 1.8 engine. As with most cars, the later the better.

GOLF MARK 2

Introduced at the tail end of 1983, the Mark 2 was bigger and better and is the pick of the bunch if you want practicality and reliability. Avoid the 1.3 and smaller engines, which were only fit for hauling Polos around. The major development for the GTI in 1986 was the 16-valve version, which boosted output from 112bhp to 139bhp. The original verdict was that it

offered few real advantages over the standard 8-valve car and had to be worked hard at high revs to extract the extra performance. The standard electric windows, central locking and higher insurance grouping hardly seem worthwhile, but they are now relatively cheap to buy.

The 1987 model year saw minor trim updates, and the windscreen wipers were belatedly aligned for right hand drive. Late 1989 saw the 'big bumper' facelift and finally the run-out October 1991 GTI got snazzy BBS alloy wheels, smoked rear lamp lenses, electric front windows, metallic paint and 16-valve interior trim.

GOLF MARK 3

Underneath the slippery new body it is essentially a Mark 2. If your priority is safety, then this is the safest Golf. Early criticisms were all about quality and the fit and finish of the cars was called into question. Volkswagen did sort out those problems under warranty, but the interior in particular can feel sub-standard when compared to a Mark 2. The 1.4 engine is underpowered. The 2.0 litre GTI is a much more refined car, though without the rawness of the original it is just a little boring. A service history is even more crucial when buying one of these much more sophisticated cars.

CONVERTIBLE

The convertible was not quite up to the GTI badge. It may have had the same engine, but it was some 12 per cent heavier, which necessitated re-jigged suspension and produced a body that could never be as rigid as the saloon. Therefore its handling characteristics are different – yet the convertible has considerable character of its own. If you want a durable, four seat approach to rag-top motoring, this is it.

From 1984 the convertibles were badged as GTIs and had the excellent 1.8 unit installed and then in 1987 the bumpers were colour keyed and wheel arch extensions fitted. An old GLi may now be cheap, but the post 1984 cars are the ones to buy. From late 1991 the GTI was replaced by model run-out special editions, the Sportline and Rivage, which were well equipped and good value. Many have been used as second cars, with lower than average mileage and less exposure to corrosive winter conditions.

SCIROCCO

Underneath it, too, is just a Golf. Unfortunately the Mark 1 body, which was universally acknowledged as a design classic, is very susceptible to rot. It is to some extent a collector's item, but it can be expensive to restore. Increasingly, minor body and trim parts are becoming difficult to find, whereas the mechanicals are everywhere. For day to day use stick with a Mark 2, which is virtually bullet proof. All Sciroccos are underrated and cheap, and the most overlooked model of all is the 16-valve model, which is very quick. This is one of the best used coupés you can buy and examples are often not as abused as their Golf GTI counterparts.

CORRADO

The Corrado offers an attractive and practical approach to running a coupé. Post 1992 models with sensible heater controls are better buys. Ensure that specialist VR6 and G60s have been looked after. The 2.0

litre 16-valve is a disappointment and many drivers prefer the earlier 1.8 version.

JETTA AND VENTO

These cars have been very underrated, especially in the UK. They will do everything that the hatchbacks do, yet that huge boot and a split rear seat means that they can cope with most loads. Go for the Mark 2 Jetta, which like the equivalent Golf was tough and virtually rust proof, with plenty of room inside. The GTI in particular is worth seeking out as it is much less likely to have been abused thanks to the dowdy Jetta image and it will be much cheaper.

It has been the same story with the Vento, which was even underplayed by Volkswagen themselves in the UK – despite having the same engine as the Golf GTI the Vento only got a GL designation.

CHECK POINTS – GOLF

Bodywork Mark 1 Golfs are the worst, even though the six year anti-corrosion warranty was effective from 1979. Look at the tops of the inner wheel arches, where the bolts attach them to the bodywork, also the sills, doors, around the sunroof, the wheel arches and the edges of the doors and tailgate. Early cars now have rotten floors and sills.

Mark 2 Golfs rarely have much rot beyond a few bubbles and it will be mainly low level stuff. Poor accident repair work is the big problem; look out for over-spray, fresh or flaking paint and underseal in the engine compartment. Watch for repairs that involve the roof, or replacement panels, bumpers or spoilers. Anything that does not correspond to the year of manufacture and 100 per cent Volkswagen-Audi

Check around doors, sills and wheelarches for corrosion on the Mark 1 Golf.

The tailgate is another area where the Mark 1 may show signs of corrosion.

build or repair quality should be questioned.

Interior The quality of the plastic mouldings and upholstery means that whatever the mileage, the view is reassuringly new. The seats may sag, an abused parcel shelf may crack and on Mark 1 Golfs the carpet may even shrink slightly, but essentially it remains as it left the factory. That can lead to clocking problems – but if

the service history does not help, a very shiny steering wheel and plastic door trim will.

Engine These last for ever, but when there is a problem it can be traced to old age when valve oil seals deteriorate and you get a smoky exhaust as a result. When healthy, the engine uses minimal amounts of oil, so a low reading on the dipstick should warn you off. A healthy Golf engine

Golf interiors are generally very hard-wearing, and should really show little sign of age.

The durability of the VW Golf engine is legendary. Check that the engine looks healthy.

looks slightly corroded, a rusty block and oxidized gearbox being testament to a leak free unit. Clattering valve gear is perfectly normal, so do not worry – it can easily be adjusted. See Scirocco for carburettor engines.

Fuel filler pipe This gets rusty and particles can foul up the injection and carburettor systems, mainly on the Mark 1 and 2.

Gearbox and drive train Clutches were a problem on pre 1981 cars before a larger component was fitted. Most should have been uprated. On right hand drive Mark 1 Golfs the bulkhead anchorage point for the clutch cable can break up and may need to be repaired. Try moving off in second gear to make sure that the clutch is intact: a heavy pedal is a sign that the clutch is on its way out. The gearbox is as durable as the engine, but in old age it can become notchy and sloppy. A common fault is for the ball to become so worn that you will select reverse as easily as first. Worn synchromesh will show up on a crunching cold second gear and reverse. Drive shafts may knock on full lock and if the gaiters have split and oil has seeped into the wheels, then they could be shot.

Suspension, brakes and tyres This is where an enthusiastically driven GTi chews through your wallet. The rear suspension is fault free, but front top mounts clunk when worn, otherwise periodic new dampers are the only items required to make a GTi handle again. As for the brakes, the discs should not be wafer thin. If in doubt, remove the wheel to check for significant scoring. The brake callipers are prone to seizure, so watch out for vague performance.

On non-power assisted cars the steering is traditionally heavy. Watch out for the seller who over inflates the front tyres to make parking easy. The tread will disappear in no time. Look for good makes of tyre rather than remoulds for a GTI. Check that the alloy wheels have not been struck heavily against a kerb, or even buckled.

Bodywork on the Convertible generally rusts in the areas of the Mark 1, but is on the whole better rust-proofed all over.

CHECK POINTS – CONVERTIBLE

Bodywork As the Golf, but the rust proofing was much improved by the time that the convertible was launched, post 1981 models being the best in this respect. Custom body kits are not good news as they can not only look awful, but also cause corrosion and affect the resale value. Check the floor area for moisture: the carpets could be hiding a corroding floor pan due to leaks or several downpours.

Engine As the Golf, but if the car has been stored for long periods look out for valve guide and seal wear, which reveals itself in blue smoke when warm and high oil consumption (check the dipstick).

Interior This is as hard wearing as most Volkswagen products but being open to the elements it can take more of a beating, especially the rear seat squabs. If there are tears and damage bear in mind that it will be very expensive to put right. Water stains will point to hood leaks.

Hood The hood is a very expensive piece of kit, so make sure you erect it and examine it carefully. Vandals or a careless owner

The interior of this boot on the convertible is immaculate, and all visible areas show little – if any – signs of wear and ageing.

can cause plenty of damage. Complete replacement is costly although localized repairs and parts can be more reasonable. Do not buy before you know the cost of putting it right.

The electric hood is a slow operator and will cost even more to sort out, so make sure you see it raised and lowered a few times. Where is the hood cover? This item has often been mislaid. Also, mist up the rear screen and switch on the heated window – the wiring or element can break due to the up and down nature of its life.

CHECK POINTS – SCIROCCO

Bodywork   Rust was always a big problem on the Mark 1. Look at the door bottoms and at the tops just below the window, then the rear wheel arches, sills and tailgate lower edges. At the front it gets more serious, especially where the wings are bolted to the inner wings. The tops of the struts do not rust too badly, but where the front panel meets the wings rust can set in with a vengeance. At the back the

rear valance disappears into a crumbly heap, but like the wings these are cheap to buy and easy to replace. Structural rust on the sills or in the floor pan means that no repair is going to be straightforward or cheap. Mark 2 Sciroccos, even early ones, should be very sound, with only cosmetic reddening of the panels.

Interior   As the Golf, but you can find though that uncaring owners have tried to stuff more than they should into the backs of the less capacious Scirocco, damaging the tailgate, lip, carpet and split rear seat.

Engine   As on the Golf, these are unbreakable units, but when they do get tired you will hear a rattle when starting from cold, which indicates worn big ends. Blue smoke from the exhaust when warm, plus a heavy oil mist when the oil cap is removed, points to worn piston rings. The pressure relief valve can be sticky; when open it leads to lack of pressure and when closed it means oil leaks (there is a warning buzzer on 1980s models when the pressure drops). On early examples the carburettors can be problematic. The 1600 twin chokes are worst and contribute to poor running and lacklustre performance. Like the GTI, the K-Jetronic system in the GLi runs very well if the servicing is up to scratch and the fuel filters are replaced regularly. Watch out for a rusty fuel filler pipe, which will eventually destroy the carburettors or the injection system.

CHECK POINTS – CORRADO

Bodywork There will only be rot if someone has repaired the bodywork poorly after a smash. However, paintwork on early examples not always perfect.
Engine As on the Golf, the strong engine holds up well unless neglected. Some starting problems have been reported. The supercharger on the G60 is intrusively noisy, especially if it rattles on tick-over. A VR6 must be quiet and smooth, with a full service history.
Transmission The gearbox bearings can get noisy with age.
Interiors These were not as well screwed together as Sciroccos, so there may be buzzes from the dashboard. The door trims are also fragile.

ADVANCED GOLFOLOGY

Volkswagen have spent millions of Deutschmarks making sure that your Golf, Scirocco, Jetta, Vento or Corrado is perfect, so why mess about with perfection? With very few exceptions the standard product that rolled out of Wolfsburg is more than adequate and unlike many other mass produced cars emerges from the factory fully formed and ready to do a couple of decades of hard work. Why not leave well alone?

But the Golf has proved to be a magnet for customizers and attention seekers. There is no shortage of parts and question-able modifications to keep them satisfied. Some people cannot bear to be lumped in with the standard specification herd and are determined to draw a crowd of their own. (The acquisition of the latest widget merely for its own sake makes them nightmare company at a cocktail party. Most are too self absorbed to be invited into the real world, but you could get stuck in the lift with one!) And finally there is the perfectionist, a role we can easily accept in an imperfect and disappointing world. Having cleverly identified a minor flaw in some aspect of our Volkswagen's performance we seek to rectify that imperfection at any cost.

Anyone who falls into those categories will not get much that they do not already know from the next few pages, but for the rest of us there might be the odd revelation, or reassurance that something can be done to sort out our Volkswagens. All the models respond well to modifications and are served by enthusiastic specialists the world over. Be warned though that this is a fast changing environment as today's state of the art engine gizmo is tomorrow's disposable piece of technological junk. Many of the products mentioned here will be out of date by the time this book is published.

While researching this book the author contacted all the best known Volkswagen performance gurus in the UK including Brian Ricketts at BR Motorsport, Tim Stiles at TSR, GTi Engineering and parts suppliers Autocavan – and you should too. Anything that goes beyond the merely cosmetic has to be done properly. If you make a Volkswagen go faster, then it makes sense that it should also stop quicker and corner better. The sensible and safe way to do this is to buy integrated performance packages along with uprated suspension and braking modifications. Although it can be done to a budget it cannot be done cheaply. Before running through what the specialists can do for each specific model, here is a simplified guide to upgrading your Volkswagen.

Bodywork Despite the aerodynamic effects of a rear wing and front splitter, unless you are an entrant for the local touring car series the performance benefits of most body modifications is minimal. The effect is purely visual. There are lots of body kit options, but make sure you can reverse the modification easily because fashions change overnight. (At the time of writing the fad is to clean up the appearance by removing badges and trim, and to paint the body in an obscenely loud colour.)

Interior Not everyone appreciates the firm seating. Specialist seats are the answer, although they are not cheap. More tactile steering wheels are an option, as are extra instruments, fancy wooden inserts and new gear knobs.

Wheels and tyres On the purely cosmetic level, a set of low profile tyres surrounding an alloy wheel will improve the looks of your Volkswagen no end. The arches look fuller and the car is much more attractive. The dynamic payoff is improved handling, grip and braking, so that driving becomes a safer and satisfying experience. A larger wheel may even expose the brakes, improving airflow and efficiency. Get it wrong, though, and the wheels could foul the arches over bumps or under a heavy load, and the ride may suffer. Expert help is essential to fit the right combination for your Volkswagen. This is a very good place to start when upgrading your car.

Suspension There is always a compromise between ride and handling. Ideally you do not want to roll around corners, or bounce wildly along a bumpy road. But set the suspension too hard and it all becomes jittery and utterly uncomfortable. So you

need to get it right and talk to a specialist to find out which set-up is best for you. There are lots of springs and damper sets on the market, some of which are adjustable to suit the conditions. Other improvements include the replacement of rubber suspension bushes with polyurethane ones to cut down road noise and locate the suspension more accurately. Anti-roll bars prevent the car from rolling, but without affecting the normal performance of the suspension. So the car stays on a flatter plane through corners, giving the driver more control, a comfortable ride and safer handling.

Chassis Volkswagens have excellent chassis, but stress bars are the answer to the flexing that occurs when the car is driven hard. Monocoque body shells, especially hatchbacks, are less rigid than saloons and can benefit from a strut, brace or bar fitted to the tops of the suspension towers, or attached to the suspension wishbones. The result is more positive steering and more assured behaviour when cornering.

Brakes Upgraded brakes are an essential prerequisite to an engine tune and well worth considering for certain early models. Fitting ventilated disc brakes with matched high performance pads is the usual route. Sometimes larger diameter discs from other models can be installed. You will stop more quickly.

Exhaust Getting gasses out of the engine is crucial to getting the most power out of a Volkswagen engine. A good manifold attached to a free-flow exhaust is the answer.

Engine Volkswagen's range of four cylinder, water cooled overhead camshaft engines have proved to be strong and consequently very susceptible to tuning. Simple modifications amount to little more than fitting a free-flow air filter, which will help the engine breathe better while

Stress bars fitted to an R&A Designs car.

keeping harmful dirt out. Increasingly modified engine management system chips form part of an engine tuning package. Sometimes the power gains are small, but the effect on the overall running and economy of the engine can be remarkable.

To the delight of tuners the absence of a cross-flowed cylinder head on the 8-valve unit in particular has left it open for development. Extra power mostly comes from the cylinder head, and the head can be modified to improve airflow by removing manufacturing imperfections such as casting lines and machined edges. In addition the head can be gas flowed, while the inlet

and exhaust valves and valve seats are re-profiled. The result is more efficient running and higher power output.

As valve timing becomes more critical with regard to output, emissions and power throttling devices like catalytic converters and sports camshafts can be added. The next step is enlarging the engine by boring out the block to increase the displacement. Ultimately you could go for the turbocharging option – not cheap, but nonetheless a highly effective way of increasing power. Simplest of all, fit a bigger engine. The interchangeability is pretty good throughout the range and it is possible to get VR6

One of the 16-valve conversions offered by GTi Engineering.

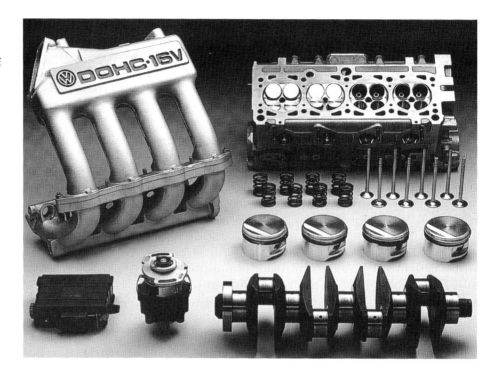

engines into Mark 2 body shells. Finally, you could just take your Volkswagen to the local dealer or specialist and get it tuned properly, as Wolfsburg intended. It is amazing how well a standard car runs.

UPGRADING SPECIFIC MODELS

The above comments merely scratched the surface of making your Volkswagen go faster. In the performance market, specialists can do much for particular models.

Golf and Jetta Mark 1 Professional tuners concentrate on the later 1.8 engine, or just install one as a straight swap and tune from there. Otherwise a 1.6 can be teased by gas flowing the cylinder head, fitting a mild sports camshaft and a decent sports exhaust.

Most drivers moan about the inadequate brakes on the Mark 1. Fortunately it is possible to improve them dramatically with a revised servo and master cylinder. Special high quality discs and branded competition pads are the finishing touches to help you stop in time.

There are still plenty of body kits available, though many are of questionable aesthetic appeal.

Golf and Jetta Mark 2 There is much potential with the 1.8 GTI engine. There are simple modifications where the head stays on and more efficient components are installed, such as sports camshaft, free flow air cleaner and a sports exhaust system for a 10 to 15bhp gain. From there larger power gains occur when the cylinder head is gas flowed for 20bhp gains and if the engine is bored out to take the capacity up to 2.0 litres then 30 to

40bhp more is possible.

There is room for improvement with the 16-valve engine too. As it is at its best when the revs are high, many conversions concentrate on improving low speed torque and driveability at low revs. Like the 8-valve, increasing the capacity by boring out the block results in the biggest power gains, although BR Motorsport offer a conversion where the 2 litre block from the Mark 3 is used to produce an engine that is more powerful than a VR6, but much more fuel efficient.

The brakes are pretty good on a Mark 2, but they can be uprated. Tim Stiles Racing offer Eurotech front discs in sizes up to 11.6in (285mm) – combined with Ferodo pads and a repositioning of the standard calliper these give excellent stopping power.

Golf and Vento Mark 3   There is plenty of room for improvements to the engine – even with the lowly 1.4 and 1.6 units, which really need a power boost to help them out. A special camshaft, re-programmed ECU chip, free flow air cleaner and sports exhaust system result in an increase of 15bhp. The same applies to the 1.8.

The 2.0 8-valve GTI engines respond well to either more efficient compression (a high lift sports camshaft, re-programmed ECU chip, free flow sports exhaust and air cleaner give 125 to 130bhp) or major cylinder head surgery (gas flowed cylinder head, inlet and exhaust manifolds, re-profiled valves and valve seats, sports camshafts, re-programmed ECU chip and free flow air cleaner give 140 to 145bhp). The 2.0 16-valve is similar – head work and sports components get it into the 170 to 175bhp region.

Even the VR6 can be improved. BR Motorsport have a conversion that adds an extra 25bhp involving sports camshafts

and high performance valve springs that boosts output by 35bhp. They also supply and fit the VSR, a variable inlet manifold. This device, designed by Volkswagen and fuel injection specialists Pierburg, gives 20bhp more power, better torque by 17 per cent at 3,500rpm and increased fuel economy.

The exhaust is rather unsatisfactory on the GTI and VR6. The simple answer is to fit a sports exhaust where the centre bore is unrestricted ('straight through' in boy racer speak). There is an increase in power and torque, but most important of all it makes a pleasing growl.

Drivers used to the relative firmness of the Mark 1 and 2 suspension can be alarmed at the way that a Mark 3 will lurch through corners. Anti-roll bar kits and stiffer heavy duty springs and dampers make all the difference.

Convertible   Anything that you can do to a Golf – tuning, engine swaps and body kits – can also be inflicted on a convertible. One conversion unique to this model is the Tonik hardtop from Vilkus: a seven piece hardtop assembly that can be used to replace the normal folding hood. Different panels can be removed to give different configurations for different weather conditions. The whole assembly can be stored in an accordion-like pouch that is packed away in the boot. The rear screen is a useful six inches wider than that of the soft top.

Scirocco   Engine modifications are as the Mark 1 and 2 Golf. The Scirocco is cheaper to buy, but is lighter, more aerodynamic and therefore more frugal and faster than the equivalent Golf. That makes a Scirocco the ideal go-faster project. Engine transplants are easy as the 2.0 litre 16-valve and G60 bolt straight in. However, the older models are limited by their carburettors; a sports camshaft, improved exhaust and gas flowing the cylinder head may be the answer.

All Sciroccos need to have their brakes uprated (as the Golf). The suspension kits available for Golfs are not always appropriate for Sciroccos as the ride can become too hard and uncomfortable.

Corrado Engine modifications are as the Golf. BR Motorsport offer a conversion for the G60 that boosts output by 19 per cent. They fit a sports camshaft, smaller supercharger pulley and belt tensioner plus a re-programmed engine management chip. The larger VR6 of the Corrado can be reworked to crack the 200bhp barrier with a revised head and boosted even further by a VSR unit.

Vento and Golf Diesel The worst model is a dull old Vento with an oil burning 1.9 diesel engine. Even so, the cylinder head can be gas flowed and the turbo boost and diesel pump timing optimized to produce anything from a 15 to 30bhp increase in dieseling output! There is also lot you can do to the bodywork to make a Vento stand out from the crowd.

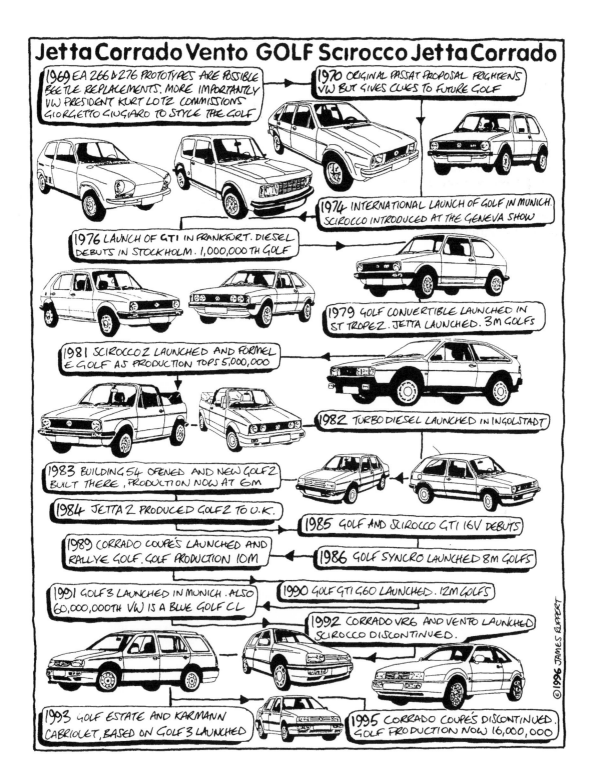

Jetta Corrado Vento GOLF Scirocco Jetta Corrado

1969 EA 266 & 276 PROTOTYPES ARE POSSIBLE BEETLE REPLACEMENTS. MORE IMPORTANTLY VW PRESIDENT KURT LOTZ COMMISSIONS GIORGETTO GIUGIARO TO STYLE THE GOLF

1970 ORIGINAL PASSAT PROPOSAL FRIGHTENS VW BUT GIVES CLUES TO FUTURE GOLF

1974 INTERNATIONAL LAUNCH OF GOLF IN MUNICH. SCIROCCO INTRODUCED AT THE GENEVA SHOW

1976 LAUNCH OF GTI IN FRANKFURT. DIESEL DEBUTS IN STOCKHOLM. 1,000,000 TH GOLF

1979 GOLF CONVERTIBLE LAUNCHED IN ST TROPEZ. JETTA LAUNCHED. 3M GOLFS

1981 SCIROCCO 2 LAUNCHED AND FORMEL E GOLF AS PRODUCTION TOPS 5,000,000

1982 TURBO DIESEL LAUNCHED IN INGOLSTADT

1983 BUILDING 54 OPENED AND NEW GOLF 2 BUILT THERE, PRODUCTION NOW AT 6M

1984 JETTA 2 PRODUCED GOLF 2 TO U.K.

1985 GOLF AND SCIROCCO GTI 16V DEBUTS

1989 CORRADO COUPÉS LAUNCHED AND RALLYE GOLF. GOLF PRODUCTION 10M

1986 GOLF SYNCRO LAUNCHED 8M GOLFS

1991 GOLF 3 LAUNCHED IN MUNICH. ALSO 60,000,000TH VW IS A BLUE GOLF CL

1990 GOLF GTI G60 LAUNCHED. 12M GOLFS

1992 CORRADO VR6 AND VENTO LAUNCHED. SCIROCCO DISCONTINUED.

1993 GOLF ESTATE AND KARMANN CABRIOLET, BASED ON GOLF 3 LAUNCHED

1995 CORRADO COUPÉS DISCONTINUED. GOLF PRODUCTION NOW 16,000,000

© 1996 JAMES RUPPERT

Useful Addresses

This list, though by no means comprehensive, gives organizations and companies that could make your Golf go better, or make ownership easier or cheaper.

Association of British Volkswagen Clubs
66 Pinewood Green, Iver,
Buckinghamshire SL0 0QH.

Autocavan (parts)
103 Lower Weybourne Lane, Badshot Lea,
Farnham, Surrey GU9 9LQ.
Telephone 01252 333891.
Branches and stockists nationwide.

Automotive Developments
(performance tuning and chips)
Oddington Garage, Oddington, Oxford.
Telephone 01865 331226.

BR Motorsport
(performance tuning, parts, service)
8A Berrington Road,
Sydenham Industrial Estate, Leamington
Spa, Warwickshire CV31 1NB.
Telephone 01926 451545.

C and R Enterprises (parts)
Units C1–4, Lake Street, Radford,
Nottingham NG7 4BT.

Club GTI
Dept VWM, PO Box 1370, Blaenau
Ffestiniog, Gwynedd LL41 4ZA.

Club VR6
Ian Johnson, 13 Saunton Close, Browns
Lane, Allesley, Coventry CV5 9EB.
Telephone 01203 402749.

Deutschcar
(performance parts and tuning)   Good
Hope Mill, Cavendish Street, Ashton-
under-Lyme, Lancashire OL6 7SL.
Telephone 0161 339 3369.

Euro Car Parts (parts)
Midland Terrace, Victoria Road,
Park Royal, London NW10 6DR.
Telephone 0181 963 0555.
Outlets also in Birmingham and
Manchester.

Eurostyling (Zender)
Telephone 0181 803 4355.

German and Swedish (parts)
Unit 2, Space Way, North Feltham
Trading Estate, Feltham, Middlesex
TW14 0TH.
Telephone 0181 893 1688.

GTi Club of South Africa
PO Box 12662, Tygerdal 7462,
South Africa.

GTi Engineering (performance tuning,
parts, service)   Oxford Road, Brackley,
Northamptonshire NN13 7DY.
Telephone 01280 700800.

Motech (performance parts)
Unit 113, Laurence Leyland Industrial
Estate, Wellingborough,
Northamptonshire NN8 1RA.
Telephone 01933 443390.

R&A Designs (body modifications)
24 Rosedale, Waltham, Grimsby,
South Humberside DN37 0UJ.
Telephone 01472 82798.

Scirocco Storm Club
Andrew Mallagh, 136 Old Heath Road,
Colchester, Essex CO1 2HB.
Telephone 01206 790328.

Scotford Ltd (Kamei)
Marriage Hill, Bidford-on-Avon,
Warwickshire B50 4EP.
Telephone 01789 772409.

TSR (performance tuning, parts, service,
sales)   5–6 Transform Estate, Wylds
Road, Bridgwater, Somerset TA6 4DH.
Telephone 01278 453036.

URO Automotive (parts)   Unit 21, Fort
Industrial Park, Dunlop Way,
Birmingham B35 7AR.
Telephone 0121 749 4700. Stockists
nation-wide.

Vilkus Hardtops (unique demountable
hardtop)   Unit 1, The Wren Centre,
Westbourne Road, Emsworth,
Hampshire PO10 7SU.
Telephone 01243 3277033.

Volks Bits (parts)
800 Pershore Road, Selly Park,
Birmingham B29 7NG.
Telephone 0121 472 4285.
Also other branches.

Volkspares Ltd (parts)
104 Newlands Park, Sydenham, London
SE26 5NA.
Telephone 0181 778 7766.
Also other branches and stockists.

Volkswagen AG   Besucherdienst 38436,
Wolfsburg, Germany.
Telephone 00 49 5361 924270.

Volkswagen Audi Car Magazine
Market Chambers, High Street,
Toddington, Bedfordshire LU5 6BY.

Volkswagen Books (mail order only)
25 Cambridge Road, Cosby, Leicester
LE9 1SH.
Telephone 0116 286 6686.

Volkswagen Motoring Magazine
PO Box 283, Cheltenham, Gloucestershire
GL52 3BT.
Telephone 01778 391000.

**Volkswagen Owners Club of Great
Britain**
PO Box 7, Burntwood, Walsall WS7 8SB.

Volkswagen UK
Yeoman's Drive, Blakelands, Milton
Keynes MK14 5AN.
Telephone 01908 679121.

Further Reading

These good Golf books helped to make this book better:

Blunsden, John, *Volkswagen Golf and Derivatives. A Collector's Guide*. MRP, 1992.

Clarke, R.M, *Volkswagen Golf GTI 1976–1986*. Brooklands Books, 1986.

Clarke, R.M, *Volkswagen Scirocco 1974–1981*. Brooklands Books, 1981.

Hutton, Ray (ed), *Volkswagen Golf GTI – The Enthusiast's Companion*. MRP, 1985.

Kuah, Ian, *Volkswagen Power and Style*. MRP, 1991.

Norbye, Jan P, *Volkswagen Treasures by Karmann*. Motorbooks International, 1985.

Vack, Peter, *Illustrated Volkswagen Buyer's Guide*. Motorbooks International, 1993.

Wagstaff, Ian, *Volkswagen Golf GTI*. Windrow and Greene Automotive, 1992.

Wagstaff, Ian, *Volkswagen Golf GTI Classics in Colour*. Windrow and Greene Automotive, 1992.

Index